A Year of
CROSS-STITCH

*M*yriad stitches, slowly wrought
Together form a lovely whole
The sewer guided, thread and thought
In harmony of hand and soul.

In its creator's patient art
The sampler's gift will best be found
Deep pleasure does this work impart
To be enjoyed the whole year 'round.

THE
JODIE DAVIS
NEEDLE ARTS SCHOOL

A Year of
CROSS-STITCH
Patterns for Every Season
· · ·

JODIE DAVIS

Photography by Tim Lee

FRIEDMAN/FAIRFAX
PUBLISHERS

A FRIEDMAN/FAIRFAX BOOK

Library of Congress Cataloging-in-Publication Data

Davis, Jodie
   A year of cross-stitch : patterns for every season/ Jodie Davis.
     p.   cm.
   Includes bibliographical references and index.
   ISBN 1-56799-217-X. -- ISBN 1-56799-213-7 (pbk.)
   1. Cross-stitch--Patterns. 2. Seasons in art. I. Title
   TT778. C76D38 1995
   746.44'3041--dc20

                                  95-1794
                                    CIP

Editor: Susan Lauzau
Art Director: Jeff Batzli
Designer: Amanda Wilson
Photography Director: Christopher C. Bain
Production Associate: Camille Lee
Illlustrator: Barbara Hennig
Photography: © Tim Lee 1995

Printed in Hong Kong and bound in China

For bulk purchases and special sales, please contact:
Friedman/Fairfax Publishers
Attention: Sales Department
15 West 26th Street
New York, New York 10010

Acknowledgments
∎ ∎ ∎

Dedicated with the utmost gratitude
To Klaus Merkle
For opening the magic door.

Acknowledgments and warmest thanks . . . .

To Jannette and Roger Jackson for their guidance, kindness, and enthusiasm;
To the GEnie cross-stitchers, my sisters in stitches; To Barbara Hennig, who sweated
the small—and large—things; To Jan Hawn, a one-woman cheering section; To Don Sullivan
for his patience with a recalcitrant computer and, more so, with this computer user;
To Eleanor Levie and Anita Veccia, who provided invaluable direction and advice;
And to the talented stitchers who brought my designs to life: Carol Collins, Evie Faichney,
Di Fane, Jim Loomis, Debbie Szuluk, Carla Ward and Kathleen Weaver.

Contents

Introduction 8

CHAPTER
1

Cross-Stitch Primer 9

CHAPTER
2

Spring 18
Spring Landscape 20
Woodland Wildflowers 22
Butterfly Lamp 26
Quilt Sign 30
Dove Sampler 38

CHAPTER
3

Summer 42
Summer Landscape 44
Quilt Design Pillows 46
Kitty in a Window 54
Victorian Porch 58
Berry Sampler 62

CHAPTER

4

Autumn 66

Autumn Landscape 68

Peppers 70

Harvest Welcome Wreath 74

Quilt Baskets 78

Village Sampler 82

CHAPTER

5

Winter 88

Winter Landscape 90

Christmas Wreath 92

Beaded Rose Purse 96

Stained Glass Angel 102

Snowflake Sampler 108

A Sampling of Small Accessories 112

Heart Charm 114

Key Ring 114

Coasters 115

Bookmark 115

Scroll Pin 116

A Summary
of Stitching Instructions 117
You Are Invited 121
Appendix: Where to Find It 122

Index 125

Introduction

▪ ▪ ▪

From the tranquillity of winter's snow flurries, the joy of an erupting spring, a bask in summer's sun, or the aromatic days of autumn, every day of the year is a day for cross-stitch.

A Year of Cross-Stitch is full of wonderful projects in a spectrum of styles and skill levels, all designed for a year full of stitching pleasure. Be sure to familiarize yourself with chapter one, the Cross-Stitch Primer, before you begin any of the projects presented here. Chapters two through five focus on spring, summer, autumn, and winter, offering a potpourri of beautiful projects that capture the spirit of each season. Each includes detailed, illustrated instructions, a complete materials list, and an easy-to-read stitching chart.

A bonus section offers a sampling of small accessories, including a bookmark and a charm, perfect for gift giving.

Finally, the appendix, Where to Find It, directs you to the sources of materials for every project in the book. If your local needlework and craft shop doesn't carry what you need, company addresses and telephone numbers are available for mail order.

Page after page, you'll find rewarding projects presented in a way that makes every minute you stitch count—and makes counting stitches fun!

Cross-Stitch Primer

. . . .

This chapter serves as a mini course in cross-
stitch. All the basics are here, from materials
and supplies to techniques and procedures.
If you're a beginner, read through this chapter
carefully and refer to it regularly as you work on a
project. Experienced stitchers may want to skim
through this chapter as a refresher course and
refer to it when necessary.
Throughout this chapter you will find helpful tips,
compliments of a network of cross-stitching friends
who share their ideas through a computer
bulletin board. Feel free to adapt any of these ideas,
and write to me in care of the publisher if you'd
like to share your own tips.

Counted cross-stitch is a rewarding hobby that can be learned in a few minutes and enjoyed for a lifetime. The few supplies required for a cross-stitch project are easy to find and inexpensive to purchase: a piece of evenweave fabric, a tapestry needle, embroidery floss, and a charted design. By following a charted design and stitching simple Xs, you can create a beautiful piece of artwork.

Floss

Six-strand cotton embroidery floss is most commonly used (and in this book, exclusively used) for cross-stitch. The project charts list color numbers for DMC, J&P Coats, and Anchor (formerly owned by Susan Bates; now owned by Coats & Clark). Floss manufacturers do not provide names for their flosses, only color numbers. My color descriptions enable you to substitute any brand.

To pull the floss from the skein, look for the little diagram on one of the paper bands that encircles the floss. This will guide you in pulling the thread from the proper end, thereby avoiding a messy tangle of thread.

Cut the floss into 18- to 22-inch (46 to 56cm) lengths unless otherwise indicated. To separate the floss, strip it: Hold the floss near the top. Pull one strand from the group all the way out. If the floss tangles, pull from the other end.

If necessary, straighten the strand and revive its shine by running it along a damp sponge. Before threading your needle, recombine the required number of strands according to the instructions for the specific project you are making.

How Many Strands to Use?

Every chart in this book instructs you as to the number of strands of floss to use. For other projects, or when substituting fabrics, consult the following chart:

Evenweave Fabric Count	Number of Plies of Floss
11	3 to 4
14	2 to 3
16	2
18	2
22	1
25	2
28	2
32	2
36	1

For backstitching, use one less strand. For DMC Flower Thread, use half the number of plies you would for floss.

Color Bleeding

Due to restrictions on the use of color-setting chemicals in dyes, some floss colors may bleed. DMC has notified stitchers that the following colors are suspect: 349; 498; 606; 666; 814; 815; 816; 817; 900; 902; 939; 946.

Before using these colors, take some precautions: Remove the labels; rinse the thread in cool water until bleeding stops; rinse in a solution of one part vinegar to two parts water; dry the thread thoroughly.

If you don't pretreat the threads and find that the colors bleed when you wash the finished needlework, keep rinsing until the water runs clear. Then rinse the needlework in the vinegar/water solution described above.

Specialty Threads

Several specialty threads are used for projects in this book.

Variegated floss from DMC comes in a variety of colors. Each skein includes gradations of a color, often with the addition of white. *Hand-dyed floss* may be one color overdyed with another shade of the same color, or it may be multiple colors dyed in sections. All can be used in a number of ways for various effects. When using variegated or hand-dyed floss, complete each cross-stitch as you go.

Blending filament is a metallic thread that is most often paired with embroidery floss to add asubtle sheen. For maximum effect, keep the blending filament on top of the floss.

Follow these tips when stitching with blending filament and other metallic threads:

■ To prevent the blending filament from fraying, apply a drop of seam sealant, such as Fray Check, to the ends. This will also make threading your needle easier.

■ Due to their slick nature, metallic threads tend to slip in the needle. To avoid this, knot the metallic thread onto the needle. Make a loop in the thread and pass it through the eye of the needle, leaving a short tail.

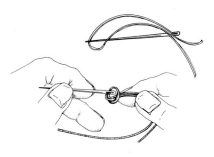

Finally, add the number of strands of floss indicated for each project.

■ Since metallic threads shred easily, using short lengths and the stab method will eliminate much of the abrading stitching will inflict. Also, using a larger needle will help by opening the hole in the fabric.

Fabrics

Counted cross-stitch is worked on specially designed fabric of even weave. Threads are woven evenly both horizontally and vertically to give the same number of threads in each direction. Crossed stitches are made over the intersections of the horizontal and vertical threads.

Cross-stitch is worked on two types of evenweave fabric: Aida and evenweave. To make evenweave fabrics, single threads are woven in a regular weave. Groups of threads are woven to make Aida, forming a weave resembling blocks. When working with evenweave, the stitcher counts and crosses over a specific number of threads, usually two. With Aida, the stitcher works the squares formed by the blocks, counting holes rather than threads.

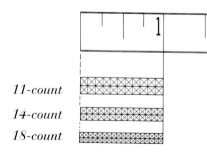

Aida is a cotton fabric available in white, ivory, and many other colors. The intersections are easy to see, making Aida perfect for beginners or for stitchers with tired eyes.

Linen and linenlike fabrics are used for heirloom-quality stitchery. For the squarest stitches, hold linen so that the selvages run vertically on the right and left. In this orientation, the straightest threads run horizontally.

Aida and evenweave fabrics are available in many thread counts and types. The count of the fabric refers to the number of threads (or, for Aida, holes) per inch (2.5cm) of fabric.

11-count	
14-count	
18-count	

For a given cross-stitch design, varying the fabric thread count will change the size of the finished design. The higher the thread count,

the smaller the design. Since you usually stitch over two threads when working with linen, a design stitched from the same chart on 14-count Aida and 28-count linen will be the same size.

Perforated Paper

Lightweight cardboard with evenly spaced perforations, perforated paper is often used for ornaments, bookmarks, and samplers. You work the paper as you would any evenweave fabric, but you should use the stab method of stitching to avoid tearing the paper (see page 15). The paper can then be cut to the desired shape. A similar effect can be achieved with perforated plastic canvas, which is more durable and flexible.

Waste Canvas

Waste canvas is a temporary grid used for guidance in stitching a design onto non-evenweave fabrics. It is often used to cross-stitch on wearables such as sweatshirts. To use waste canvas, cut it an inch or two (2.5 to 5cm) larger than the design you've selected. Baste the canvas to the fabric in the desired location and stitch the design over the canvas. When you are finished stitching, wet the waste canvas and remove the strands one by one. A pair of tweezers is helpful for this task.

Needles

Tapestry needles are used for cross-stitch. This needle has a large eye to accommodate multiple strands of floss. The blunt-pointed tip slips between the strands, not through them. The following chart suggests which size needle is most appropriate for a specific evenweave fabric. The instructions for each project also specify needle size.

Fabric Thread Count	*Needle Size*
11	24
14	24
16	24 or 26
18 linen	24 or 26
28 linen	26
30 linen	26

For perforated paper, stitch the design using a size 24 tapestry needle and three strands of embroidery floss. Change to a size 26 tapestry needle to do the backstitching, and your work will go much more quickly.

Hoops and Such

Counted cross-stitch can be worked with a hoop or a scroll frame, or simply held in the hand. For linen, use a stretcher frame or hold the work in your hand to avoid the distortion of fabric threads that could be caused by a hoop.

Preparing Fabric

As a general rule, cut your fabric 3 to 4 inches (7.5 to 10 cm) larger than the design all around. The optimal size to cut your fabric is designated for each project in this book.

To prevent raveling, whipstitch or zigzag stitch the edges of the fabric. Do not use tape; it will leave a residue that can creep into the stitched area and ruin your treasured heirloom.

Find the center of the charted design by following the path indicated by the arrows on the chart: the center of the design is where those two paths meet. Next, find the center of the fabric by folding it in half from left to right and in half from top to bottom: mark this point with a pin. To guide your stitching, you may wish to mark the horizontal and vertical center lines of the fabric with basting stitches of regular sewing thread in a light color. It's very helpful to baste additional lines every ten spaces both horizontally and vertically, forming a grid. This will save you counting time as you stitch.

Many stitchers prefer to start stitching at the top of the design. Once you find the centers of both the design and the fabric, simply count the squares to the top. This assures that you will always be pushing your needle up through an empty hole, which is easier and makes your work look neater. Coming up through a hole already stitched often brings fuzzy bits of thread along with it.

While stitching, you may find the floss twisting. Drop the needle and let it untwist. You want your threads to lie smooth and flat.

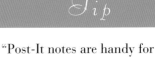
Reading the Design

Charted designs, also called graphs, are the key to cross-stitch. The chart consists of a grid, which corresponds to the threads or groups of threads of the evenweave fabric. Each square represents a block of threads; each symbol within a square represents one cross-stitch. Accompanying the chart is a list of symbols that shows which color embroidery floss each symbol represents.

Where to Begin

I prefer to begin stitching at the top of the design, working left to right. Some stitchers start at the middle of the graph, stitch the bottom half of the chart, and then turn both the graph and the fabric upside down and stitch from the middle to the top of the chart. This technique has its advantages and disadvantages: It will guarantee that your work will be centered on the fabric, but the counting becomes more tedious, since half of it is done upside down.

Beginning and Ending Stitching

Begin your stitching by securing the thread using one of the following three methods. A knot is not acceptable as it will show beneath the fabric. The tiny bumps will detract from the appearance of the finished design.

WORKING OVER THE THREAD TAIL METHOD: Cut the floss into an 18- to 22-inch (46 to 56cm) length. From the back of the fabric come up at the number 1 hole of your first stitch. Leave a tail of thread about 1 inch (2.5cm) long. Hold the thread at the back and stitch your first few stitches over it.

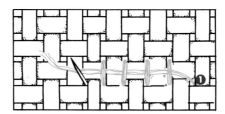

View is from back of work.

WASTE KNOT METHOD: An alternative is to make a knot in the end of the thread. Enter the fabric from the right side several inches from the location of your first stitch. When you are finished stitching with that strand of floss, clip the knot, thread the tail on your needle, and anchor it in the stitching at the back of the piece as described under To End a Thread.

LOOP METHOD: This method works only if the instructions call for an even number of strands of floss. If, for example, two plies are indicated, cut one strand of floss 36 inches (91.5cm) long. Fold the strand in half. Thread the needle with the two cut ends. Bring the needle up at the starting point, leaving the loop at the back of the fabric.

Stitch through the loop on the downward stitch, tightening the loop snugly against the fabric.

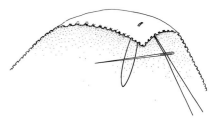

To End a Thread, complete your last stitch by bringing the floss through to the back of the fabric. Run the needle through five or six stitches at the back of your work. Clip off the excess floss.

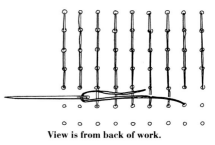

View is from back of work.

To Add a New Thread, run the needle under previous stitches on the back of the fabric or use the loop method.

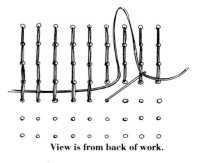

View is from back of work.

Cross-Stitching

A cross-stitch on Aida is worked differently than one in linen.

AIDA: A single cross-stitch on Aida consists of two motions: bringing the needle up from the underside, then bringing it down again from the top side. This is called stab stitching. A complete cross-stitch consists of two sets of such motions.

Start at the bottom left of the first cross-stitch, marked 1 on the diagram. Go into the fabric at 2. This is half of one cross-stitch.

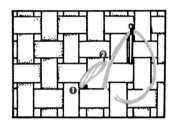

Come back up at 3 and then go back into the fabric at 4. You have now completed one full cross-stitch.

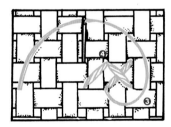

LINEN: Linen is stitched using the sewing method. Having come up at 1, make the first half of the stitch by going into the fabric at 2 and coming up at 3 in one motion rather than the two motions used in the stab method. Complete the cross-stitch, going back down at 4.

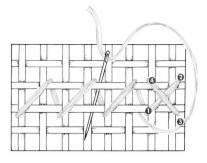

Designs on linen are most often stitched over two threads. Each stitch crosses over two threads diagonally and horizontally; up two and over two. For each square on the chart, count up two threads and over two threads.

For a nice looking, well-anchored stitch on linen-type fabrics, begin and end your stitches to the left of a vertical thread, just below and to the right of where it crosses over a horizontal thread.

Count threads, not holes. At first this will be difficult, but as you stitch it you'll find it easier and easier!

If the design calls for a row of cross-stitches, make the first halves of the stitches first, working left to right, and then cross them, working right to left.

For vertical rows, complete each stitch before going on to the stitch below.

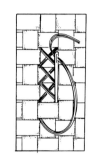

Carrying Threads

Often a color appears in adjacent areas. When you finish stitching in one area you can carry the thread over to the next area. However, you should never carry the floss more than four threads across open fabric. Instead, end the thread and start again. Be careful if you carry dark-colored floss behind a light-colored fabric—it *will* show!

Backstitch

Backstitching defines and outlines cross-stitch, details design elements, and gives the piece a finished look. Backstitches are worked after completing all the cross-stitches and, worked from hole to hole, can go vertically, horizontally, or diagonally.

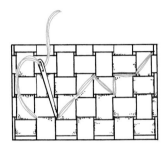

Backstitching is represented on charts as black straight lines.

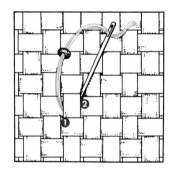

French Knots

French knots are pretty, decorative stitches. To make one, refer to the diagram and bring your needle up at 1. Wrap floss around the needle twice and go down a scant ⅛ inch (3mm) away, at 2. French knots appear on charts as dots, and are placed at an intersection of lines so as not to confuse them with cross-stitch symbols.

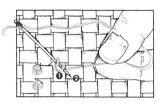

Stitching with Beads

Small seed beads worked on half cross-stitches replace complete cross-stitches in some projects. Any needle that will fit through the hole in the bead will do. Use two strands of floss. (Match the background

fabric if you wish the bead to be visually dominant.) Bring the thread up at 1 and pick up a bead. Insert the needle into the fabric at 2. This completes the half cross-stitch.

To securely anchor beads and keep them vertical, complete the cross-stitch by going back through the bead.

Mistakes

If you make an error, unstitch. Anchor the end of the floss on the back of your work and correct the error with new floss. You will not want to reuse the floss, as it will be fuzzy and rough.

Finishing

Wash your finished cross-stitch project in cool water and mild soap such as baby shampoo or clear dishwashing liquid. Cleaning will remove any oils from your hands or soil that may be on the stitched piece. Rinse thoroughly. If floss should bleed onto the fabric, keep rinsing until the water runs clear (see page 11 for instructions on setting dyes).

Never twist or wring your finished project: this will distort the fabric threads. Instead, blot the piece with a soft white towel. Lay it right side down on a white terry towel. Do not hang or machine dry. Use a dry iron set on cotton and press the finished piece until it's dry. Wrinkles will be removed, and thanks to the towel, the stitches will not be flattened. When pressing a piece stitched with blending filament, use a press cloth; otherwise the heat may melt the polyester viscose of the blending filament.

Framing

Consult your local framing or art supply shop for picture mats and frames. Beveled edges, contrasting color cores, double mats, contoured shapes, and special textures are all lovely options. All framing for *A Year of Cross-Stitch* was done by Old Town Needlecrafts (see Where to Find It).

Tip

"I use a scroll frame for most projects and frame the work so the design is under rather than over the scroll. In addition, I hold a white cotton handkerchief under my left hand where I grip the frame. This greatly reduces the amount of dirt and oil that is transferred to the linen."

*Mary Flower,
New York, New York*

Spring

. . . .

Ah, spring. The season of infinite possibility,

of new growth, fresh beginnings, delicate

colors, and sweet fragrances.

Soon the lady's slippers will grace the earth below

the hemlocks and birches in my mother's

New Hampshire woods. I have my fingers crossed,

hoping that my persnickety wisteria will bloom

at home in Virginia.

Spring is the time for the airing of quilts, for catching

sight of butterflies, for the bloom of true love. These

are the visions of spring I'd like to share with you. My

wish is that stitching these designs will fill you with the

joy and promise that is spring.

Spring Landscape

The first of a four-piece series of designs depicting a log cabin through the seasons,
Spring Landscape captures the promise of a new season.

■ ■ ■ ■ ■ ■ ■ ■ ■ ■

SIZE: Framed, $10\frac{1}{2} \times 9\frac{1}{2}$ inches (26.5 × 24cm); design area, $5 \times 3\frac{7}{8}$ inches (13 × 10cm)

FABRIC: Stitched on 14-count white Aida over one thread

STITCH COUNT: 70×55

YOU WILL NEED:

■ 14-count white Aida from Charles Craft, cut 11 inches (28cm) square
■ Six-strand embroidery floss as listed in color key, one skein each
■ Tapestry needle size 24

OPTIONS:

Fabric	Design Size
Aida 11	$6\frac{3}{8} \times 5$ inches (16 × 13cm)
Aida 16	$4\frac{3}{8} \times 3\frac{1}{2}$ inches (11 × 9cm)
Aida 18	$3\frac{7}{8} \times 3$ inches (10 × 7.5cm)

INSTRUCTIONS: Cross-stitch using two strands of floss and work over one thread of fabric.

FRAMING OPTION: Paint pussy willows in the lower right corner of the outer mat. Insert in a frame with an $8\frac{3}{4} \times 7\frac{3}{4}$-inch (22 × 19.5cm) opening, using a double mat.

Color Key

SYMBOL	DMC	ANCHOR	COATS	COLOR
Cross-stitch with 2 strands:				
0	782	308	5308	Topaz, dark
X	844	1041	8501	Beaver Brown, ultra dark
A	975	355	5356	Golden Brown, dark
V	433	358	5471	Brown, medium
&	3787	—	—	Brown-gray
<	White	2	1001	White
∿|	3777	1015	2339	Terra-cotta, very dark
z	816	1005	3021	Garnet
U	834	874	2874	Golden Olive, very light
v	3024	397	8397	Brown-gray, very light
□	758	882	2337	Terra-cotta, very light
~	827	160	7159	Blue, very light
▮	743	302	2294	Yellow, medium
#	904	258	6258	Parrot Green, very dark
s	905	257	6258	Parrot Green, dark
■	906	256	6256	Parrot Green, medium
○	895	1044	6021	Hunter Green, very dark
=	208	110	4301	Lavender, very dark
▲	937	268	6268	Avocado Green, medium
◎	3607	87	4087	Plum, light
▨	321	9046	3500	Christmas Red
?	307	289	2288	Lemon

Spring Landscape sampler pictured on page 18.

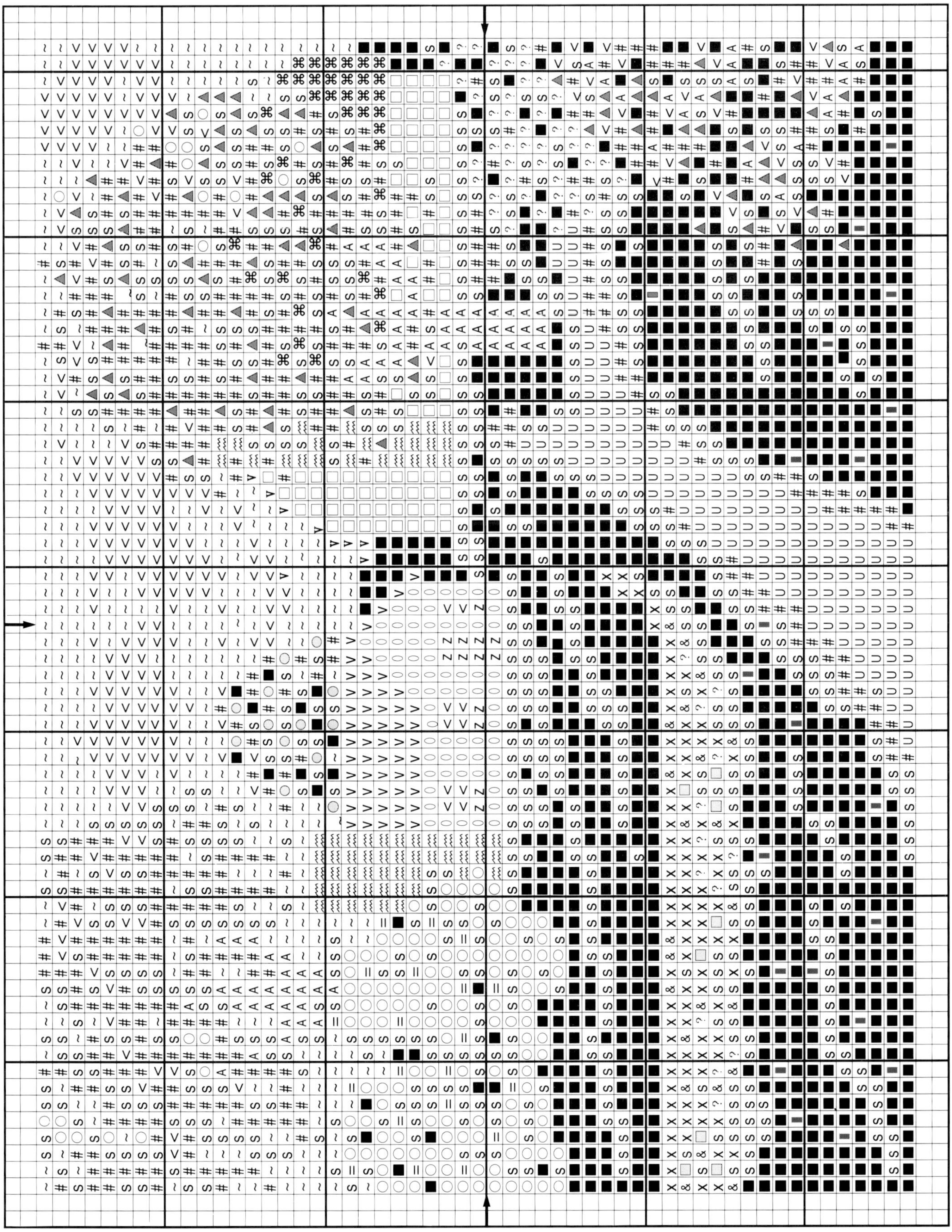

Woodland Wildflowers

Each spring, I am inspired by the miraculous appearance of delicate blossoms, even after the harshest of winters. This design is stitched with the soft colors of nature's springtime palette.

■ ■ ■ ■ ■ ■ ■ ■ ■

SIZE: Framed, $10\frac{3}{4} \times 12\frac{3}{4}$ inches (27×32cm); design area $4\frac{3}{4} \times 6\frac{3}{4}$ inches (12×17cm)

FABRIC: Stitched on 28-count cream Irish linen over two threads

STITCH COUNT: 67×97

YOU WILL NEED:

■ 28-count cream Irish linen from Charles Craft, cut 11×13 inches (28×33cm)

■ Six-strand embroidery floss as listed in color key, one skein each

■ Tapestry needle size 26

OPTIONS:

Fabric	Design Size
Aida 14	$4\frac{3}{4} \times 7$ inches (12×18cm)
Aida 18	$3\frac{3}{4} \times 5\frac{3}{8}$ inches (9.5×13.5cm)
Linen 25	$5\frac{3}{8} \times 7\frac{3}{4}$ inches (13.5×19.5cm)
Linen 32	$4\frac{1}{4} \times 6\frac{1}{8}$ inches (11×15.5cm)

INSTRUCTIONS: Cross-stitch over two threads using two strands of floss.

Backstitch using one strand of floss. Backstitch the butterflies' antennae and make French knots at the tips.

FRAMING OPTION: Use a frame with a $9\frac{1}{2} \times 11\frac{1}{2}$-inch ($24 \times 29$cm) opening. Cut mat opening to $5\frac{1}{4} \times 7\frac{1}{4}$ inches (13×18.5cm); cover

Color Key

SYMBOL	DMC	ANCHOR	COATS	COLOR
Cross-stitch with 2 strands:				
β	437	362	5942	Tan, light
#	3011	846	6845	Khaki Green, dark
2	3722	1027	3241	Shell Pink, medium
3	221	897	3243	Shell Pink, very dark
≈	335	38	3283	Rose
&	326	59	3401	Rose, very deep
■	899	52	3282	Rose, medium
8	White	2	1001	White
+	470	267	6010	Avocado Green, light
○	469	267	6261	Avocado Green
>	937	268	6268	Avocado Green, medium
=	471	266	6266	Avocado Green, very light
▼	211	342	4303	Lavender, light
/	210	108	4303	Lavender, medium
?	208	110	4301	Lavender, very dark
A	3746	1030	—	Blue-violet, dark
C	307	289	2288	Lemon
D	819	271	3280	Baby Blue, light
%	772	259	6250	Pine Green, light
□	3362	263	6317	Pine Green, dark
K	3363	262	6316	Pine Green, medium
L	3364	260	6266	Pine Green
Backstitch with 1 strand:				
—	434	310	5000	Brown, light (antennae for butterfly)

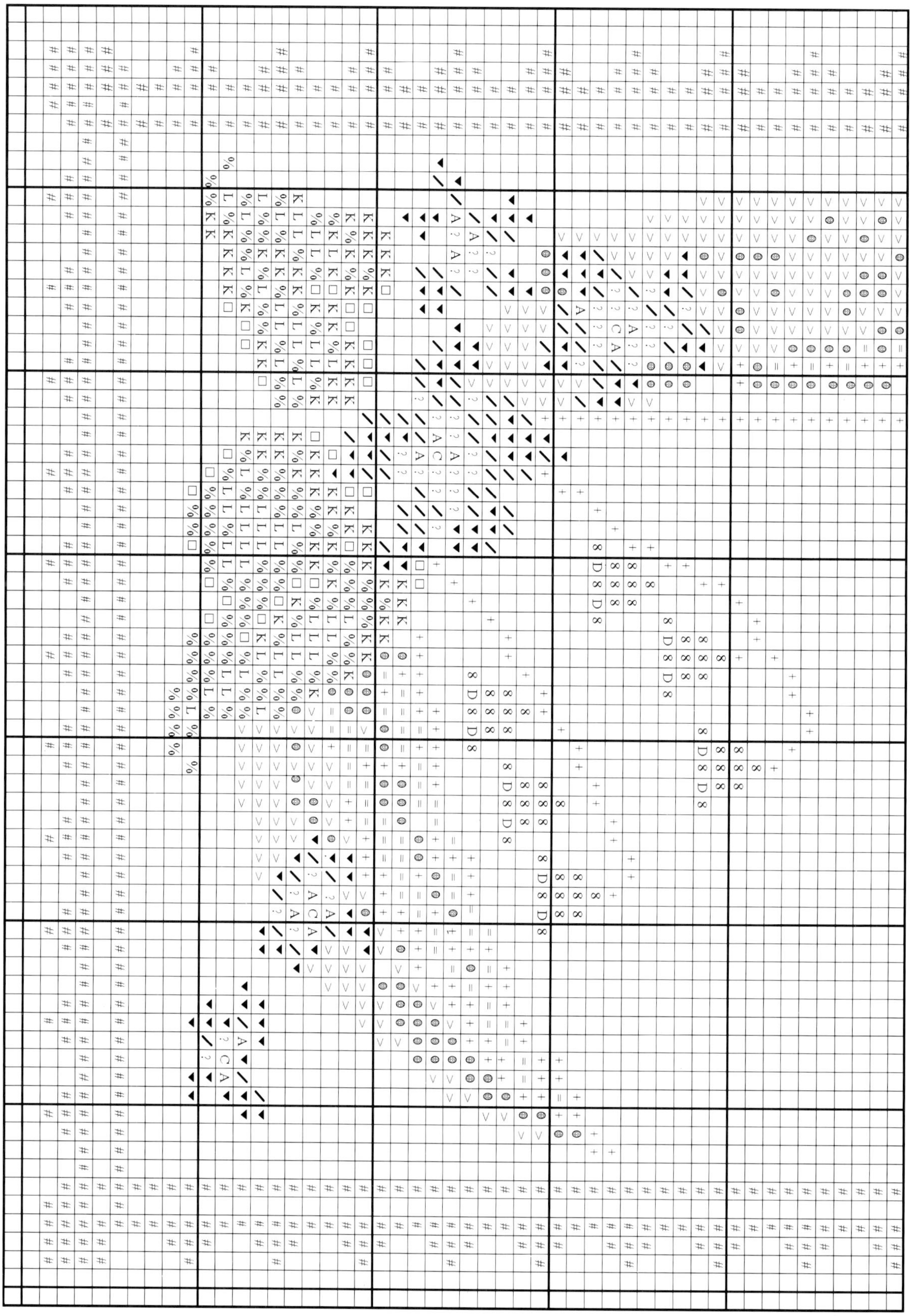

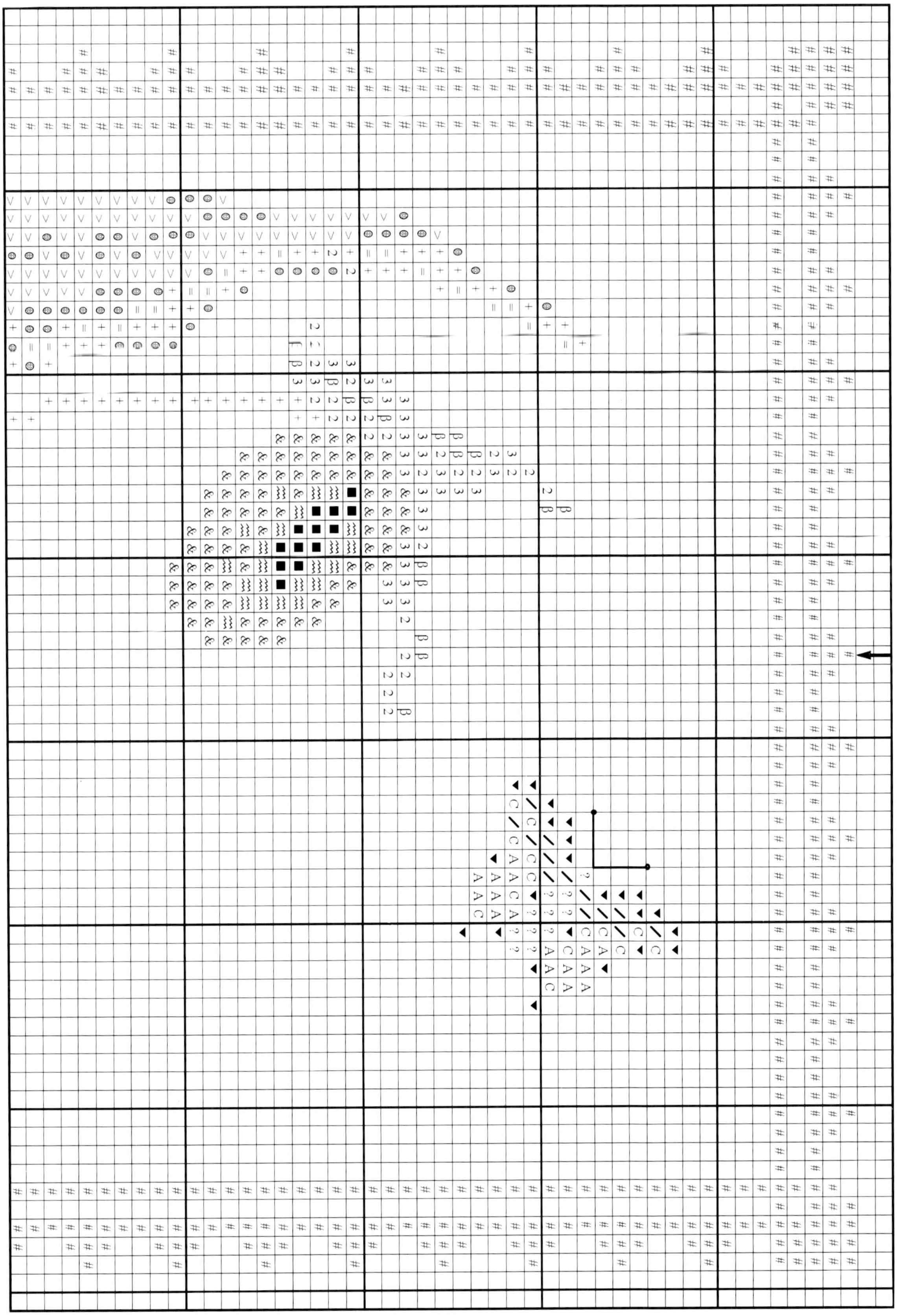

Butterfly Lamp

Butterflies and ladybugs flit among the flower borders in this animated design. A lamp base kit makes quick work of mounting the needlework in an unusual way.

■ ■ ■ ■ ■ ■ ■ ■ ■

SIZE: Lamp base to bulb, 12½ inches (32cm) tall; finished needlework, 14 × 6½ inches (3.5 × 16.5cm); design area, 12¼ × 4⅞ inches (31 × 12.5cm)

FABRIC: Stitched on 14-count black Aida over one thread

STITCH COUNT: 171 × 68

YOU WILL NEED:

■ 14-count black Aida from Charles Craft, cut 18 × 11 inches (46 × 28cm)
■ Six-strand embroidery floss as listed in color key, one skein each
■ DMC Embroidery Metallic embroidery thread as listed in color key, one skein each
■ Tapestry needle size 24
■ Lamp base from The Woodshapers Co. (see Where to Find It)
■ Lampshade

Color Key

SYMBOL	DMC	ANCHOR	COATS	COLOR
Cross-stitch with 2 strands:				
V	972	298	2298	Canary, deep
○	973	297	2290	Canary, bright
M	915	1029	—	Plum, dark
●	718	88	4089	Plum
▓	904	258	6258	Parrot Green, very dark
+	210	108	4303	Lavender, medium
◉	208	110	4301	Lavender, very dark
□	333	119	—	Blue-violet, very dark
—				DMC Light Gold metallic embroidery thread
Backstitch with 1 strand:				
▬				DMC Light Gold metallic embroidery thread

OPTIONS:

Fabric	Design Size
Aida 11	15½ × 6⅛ inches (39.5 × 15.5cm)
Aida 16	10⅝ × 4¼ inches (27 × 11cm)
Aida 18	9½ × 3¾ inches (24 × 9.5cm)
Linen 25	13⅝ × 5½ inches (34.5 × 14cm)

INSTRUCTIONS: Cross-stitch over one thread using two strands of floss. Use the metallic thread to cross-stitch the spots on the ladybugs' backs. Backstitch the ladybug and the butterfly body and antennae with the metallic thread. Assemble as instructed by the lamp manufacturer.

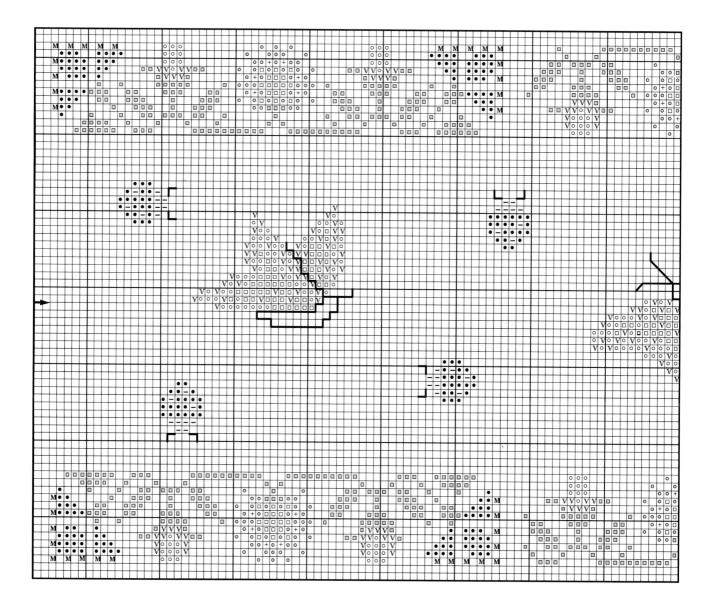

Butterfly Lamp

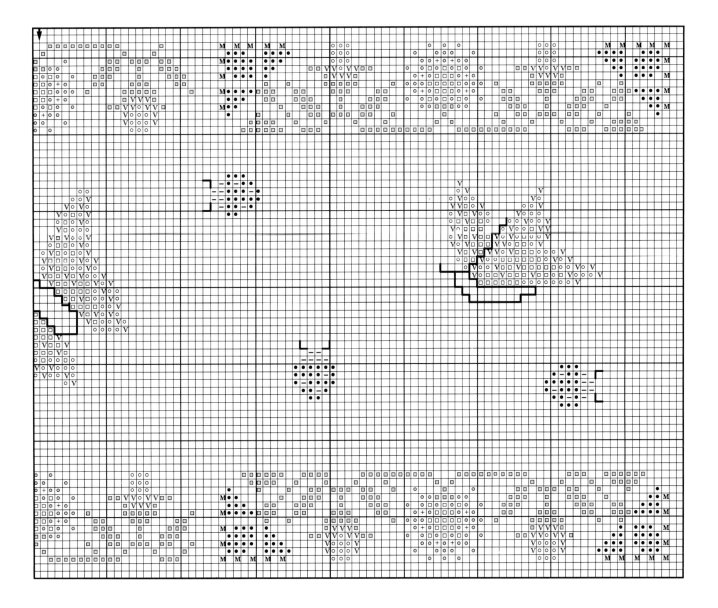

Quilt Sign

Show off your love of quilts with this cheerful announcement. The quilts are hung clothesline style, blowing in a make-believe breeze.

■　■　■　■　■　■　■

Sign

SIZE: Framed, 20½ × 13 inches (52 × 33cm); design area, 13½ × 5½ inches (34.5 × 14cm)

FABRIC: Stitched on 28-count tea-dyed linen

STITCH COUNT: 190 × 78

YOU WILL NEED:

■ 28-count tea-dyed linen from Charles Craft, cut 20 × 11 inches (51 × 28cm)

■ Flower Thread as listed in color key, one skein each

■ Tapestry needle size 26

■ ⅝ yard (57cm) of ⅛-inch (3mm) double-faced pink satin ribbon

■ 6 mini wooden clothespins

OPTIONS:

Fabric	Design Size
Aida 11	17¼ × 5½ inches (44 × 14cm)
Aida 16	11⅞ × 4⅞ inches (30 × 12.5cm)
Aida 18	10½ × 4⅜ inches (26.5 × 11cm)
Linen 25	15¼ × 6¼ inches (38.5 × 16cm)

INSTRUCTIONS: Cross-stitch using two strands of floss and work over two threads of fabric.

FRAMING OPTIONS: Insert in a frame with an 18½ × 10¾-inch (47 × 27cm) opening. Use a contoured double mat.

Quilts

SIZES: Schoolhouse, 3 × 3¼ inches (7.5 × 8cm); Irish Chain, 3 × 3½ inches (7.5 × 9cm); Trip 'Round the World, 3¼ inches (8cm) square.

YOU WILL NEED:

■ Three 7-inch (18cm) squares of cream Aida: one 14-count, two 18-count

■ Six-strand embroidery floss as listed in color key, one skein each

■ Tapestry needle size 24

■ Fabric stiffener

INSTRUCTIONS: Cross-stitch each quilt, using 14-count Aida for Trip 'Round the World and 18-count Aida for the Schoolhouse and Irish Chain designs. Trim to about 1 inch (2.5cm) from outside edge of stitching. Saturate each quilt in fabric stiffener. Squeeze out excess liquid by running the fabric between two fingers, and set it on waxed paper to dry. Before the quilt dries completely, gently bend it so it looks as if it is blown by a breeze. Allow the quilt to finish drying. Cut away excess fabric, up to the stitching. Hang with mini clothespins on a ribbon "clothesline." Make knots near the ends of the clothesline and use pins to tack it to the sign fabric after framing is completed.

Schoolhouse Quilt Color Key

SYMBOL	DMC	ANCHOR	COATS	COLOR
Cross-stitch with 2 strands over 1 thread:				
□	814	45	3044	Garnet, dark
●	820	134	7024	Royal Blue, very dark

Irish Chain Quilt Color Key

SYMBOL	DMC	ANCHOR	COATS	COLOR
Cross-stitch with 2 strands over 1 thread:				
▨	3755	140	7976	Baby Blue
╱	604	55	3001	Cranberry, light

Trip 'Round the World Quilt Color Key

SYMBOL	DMC	ANCHOR	COATS	COLOR
Cross-stitch with 2 strands over 1 thread:				
ɪ	995	410	7010	Electric Blue, dark
⌘	820	134	7024	Royal Blue, very dark
○	973	297	2290	Canary, bright
◉	550	102	4107	Violet, very dark
❖	700	228	6227	Christmas Green, bright
□	321	9046	3500	Christmas Red
■	310	403	8403	Black

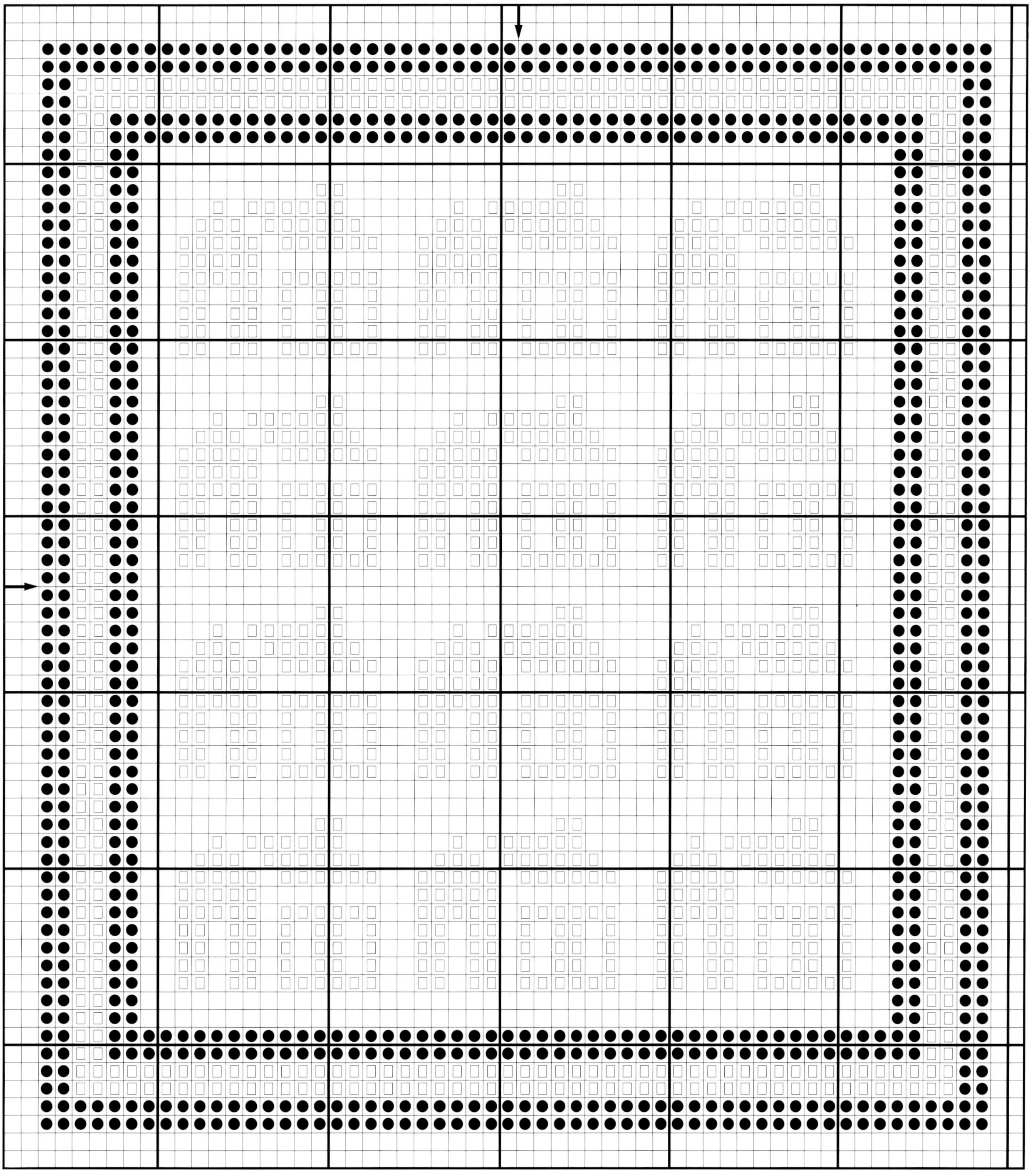

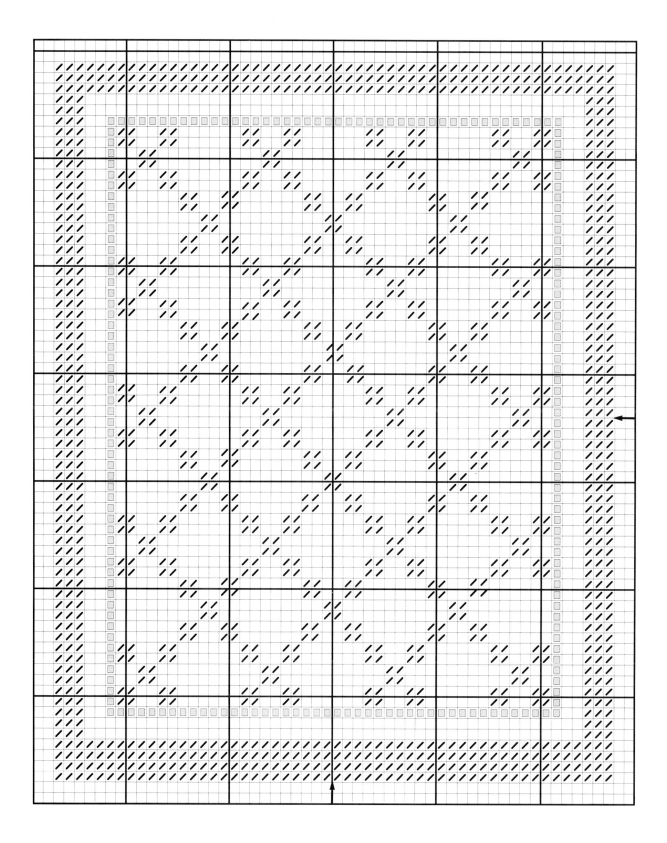

Irish Chain Quilt

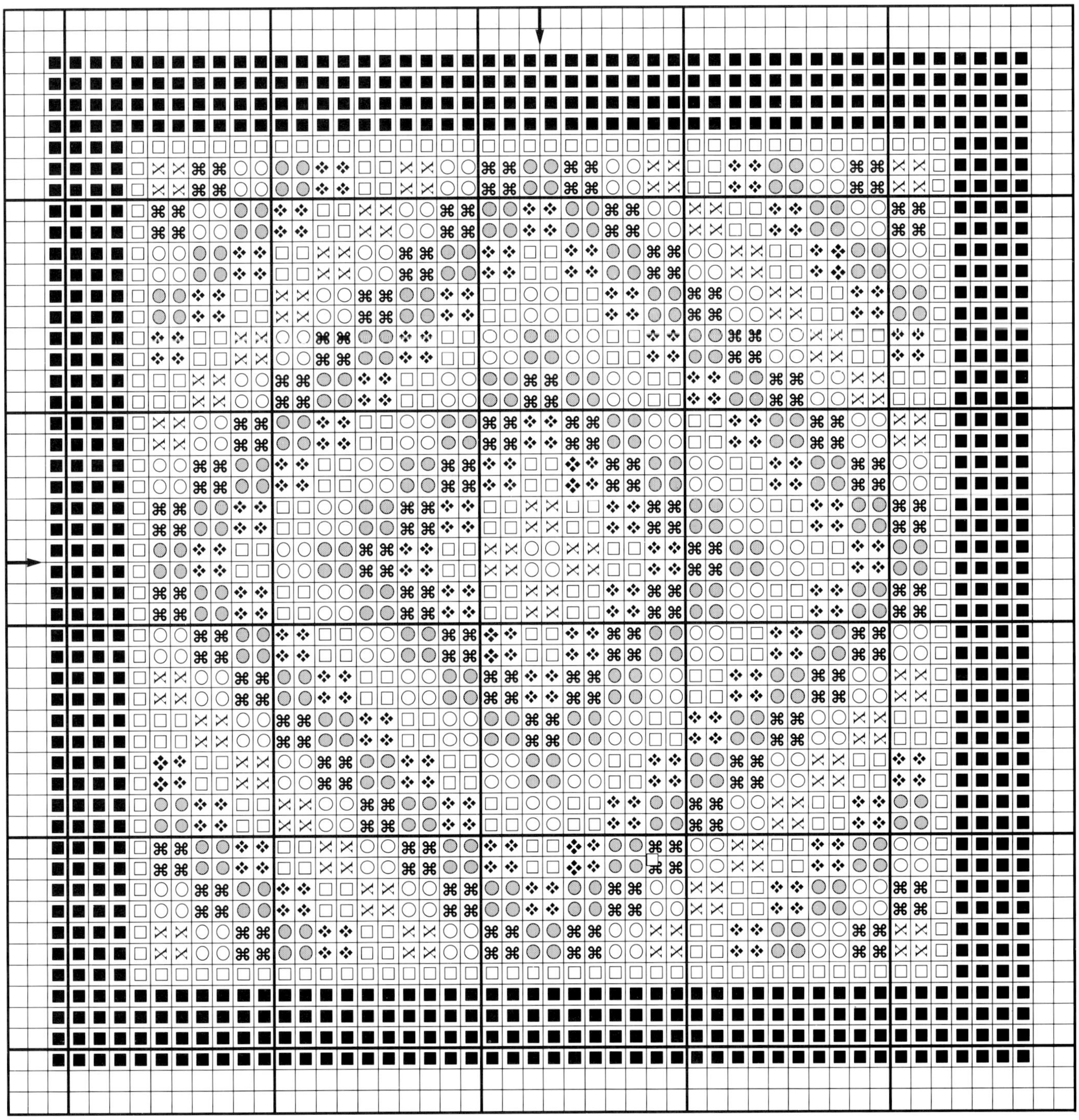

Dove Sampler

An arbor heavy with wisteria blossoms heralds spring in this romantic sampler.
Using overdyed floss promises subtle shading.

■ ■ ■ ■ ■ ■ ■ ■

SIZE: Framed, 15¼ × 13¼ inches (38.5 × 33.5cm); design area, 8⅜ × 6⅜ inches (21 × 16cm)

FABRIC: Stitched on 30-count silvery green Shannon

STITCH COUNT: 128 × 97

YOU WILL NEED:

■ 30-count silvery green shannon no. 716-23 from Wichelt, cut 16 × 13 inches (40.5 × 33cm)
■ Needle Necessities (NN) Overdyed Floss as listed in color key
■ Six-strand embroidery floss as listed in color key
■ Tapestry needle size 26

OPTIONS:

Fabric	Design Size
Aida 14	9⅛ × 7 inches (23 × 18cm)
Aida 18	7⅛ × 5¼ inches (18 × 13cm)
Linen 25	10¼ × 7¾ inches (26 × 19.5cm)

Color Key

SYMBOL	DMC	ANCHOR	COATS	NN	COLOR
Cross-stitch with 2 strands over 2 threads:					
⁓				133	Green
◊				131	Light Green
∧				110	Light Blue
S				174	Light Lavender
#				175	Purple-blue
0				176	Lavender
△				195	Dark Purple
▣				105	White
%	840	379	5379		Beige-brown, medium
▮	839	360	5360		Beige-brown, dark
+	White	2	1001		White
⊙	209	109	4303		Lavender, dark
=	211	342	4303		Lavender, light
>	554				Violet, light
Half cross-stitches with 2 strands:					
/	White	2	1001		White (trellis)
French knots with 2 strands:					
U	799	136	7030		Delft, medium (bottom border flower petals)
●	727	293	2289		Topaz, very light (bottom border flower petals)
x	3022	393	5393		Brown-gray, medium (birds' eyes)
Backstitch with 1 strand:					
—	3022	393	5393		Brown-gray, medium (dove)
—				195	Dark Purple (letters)
Backstitch the flowers in the bottom border with 2 strands, 1 each of the 2 following colors:					
—	320	215	6017		Pistachio Green, medium
—	367	217	6018		Pistachio Green, dark

INSTRUCTIONS: Stitch over two threads of fabric. Backstitch the doves and letters as indicated on the chart. Make French knots for the flowers in the lower border. Make French knots for the birds' eyes.

FRAMING OPTION: Use a double mat with a 10 × 6¾-inch (25.5 × 17cm) opening, with an arch cut over the center 4¾ inches (12cm) of the top edge. Frame has a 12 × 14-inch (30.5 × 35.5cm) opening.

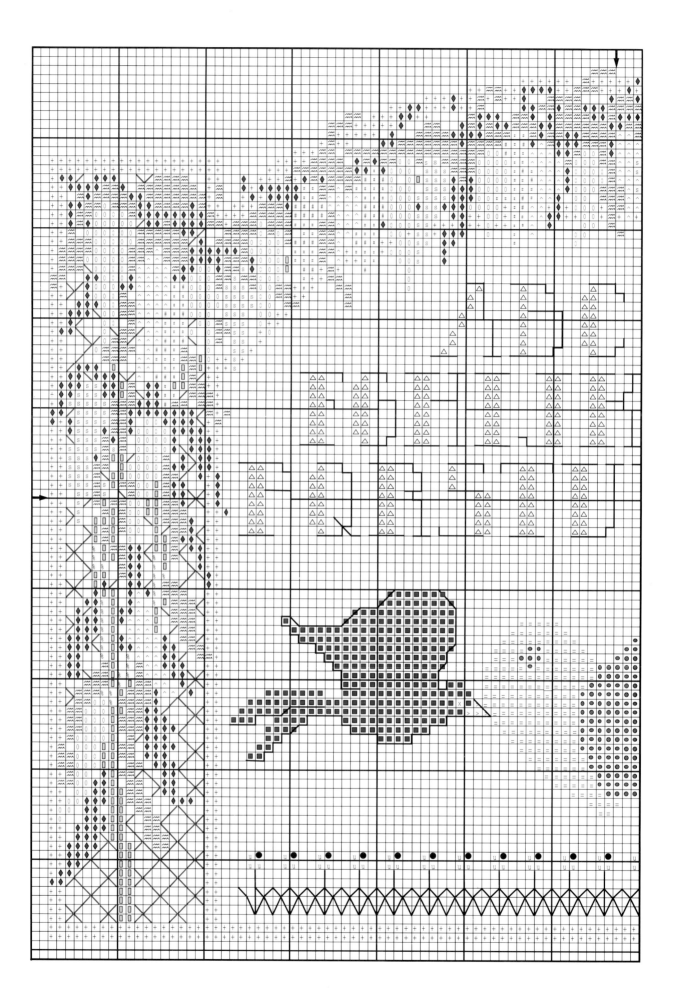

Dove Sampler

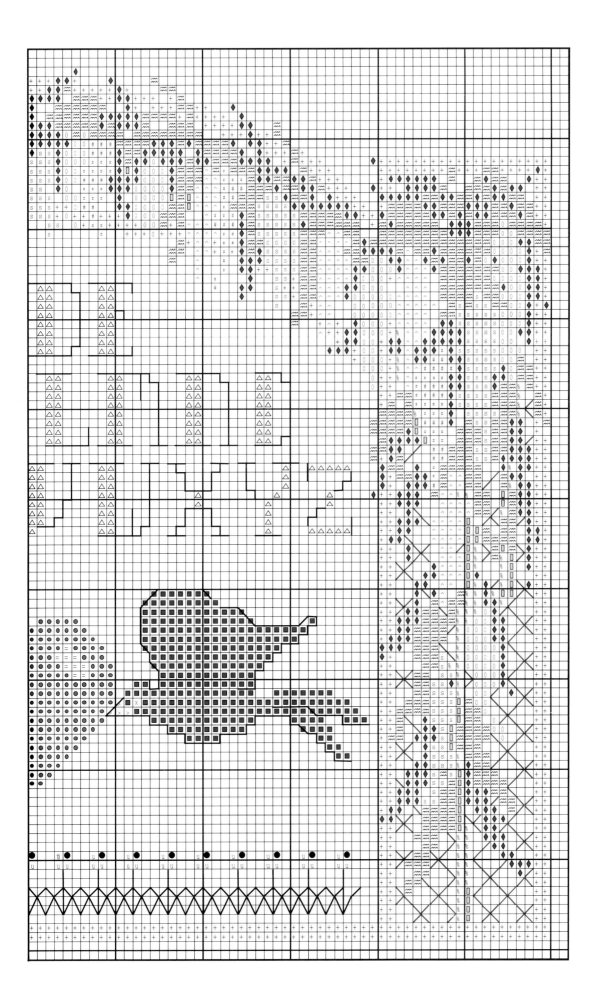

Dove Sampler

$\mathcal{S}ummer$

▪ · · · · ▪ · ▪ · ▪ · · · ▪

The rush of spring past, summer is a season to
savor. Raspberries and lemonade served in the cool
of a shaded porch epitomize this interlude between
the sowing and the harvest—a perfect time to stitch
remembrances of long, lovely summer days.

Have you guessed? That's my log cabin depicted in
each of the four seasons. This time it's shown with
my beloved clematis smothering the front porch!

A visit will surely provide a view of one of our four
cats sleeping in a window box; the kitty who gazes out
of the window in the three-dimensional, framed piece
was inspired by my own cuddly pet. The cool blue
and white pillows with daisy and heart motifs have
the homey quality of a favorite quilt, and the
Victorian Porch design couldn't be easier!

The Berry Sampler uses luscious hand-painted
threads to achieve seemingly complex shadings
over a sunny yellow background.

Linger over these cross-stitch designs on your summer
porch—whether real or imagined.

Summer Landscape

The long days of summer have set in at our log cabin home. Wild cornflowers and Queen Anne's lace make a happy marriage along the roadside. Purple-flowered clematis draperies shade the front porch, where, perhaps, a cool pitcher of lemonade waits to refresh visitors.

■ ■ ■ ■ ■ ■ ■ ■ ■ ■ ■

SIZE: Framed, 10½ × 9½ inches (26.5 × 24cm); design area, 5 × 3⅞ inches (13 × 10cm)

FABRIC: Stitched on 14-count white Aida

STITCH COUNT: 70 × 55

YOU WILL NEED:

- 14-count white Aida from Charles Craft, cut 11 inches (28cm) square
- Six-strand embroidery floss as listed in color key, one skein each
- Tapestry needle size 24

OPTIONS:

Fabric	Design Size
Aida 11	6⅜ × 5 inches (16 × 13cm)
Aida 16	4⅜ × 3¼ inches (11 × 8cm)
Aida 18	3⅞ × 2¾ inches (10 × 7cm)

INSTRUCTIONS: Cross-stitch using two strands of floss and work over one thread of fabric.

FRAMING OPTION: Paint seasonal flowers in lower left corner of outer mat. Insert in a frame with an 8¾ × 7¾-inch (22 × 19.5cm) opening. Use a double mat.

Color Key

SYMBOL	DMC	ANCHOR	COATS	COLOR
Cross-stitch with 2 strands:				
I	844	1041	8501	Beaver Brown, ultra dark
0	782	308	5308	Topaz, dark
+	3787	—	—	Brown-gray
≈	White	2	1001	White
=	3777	1015	2339	Terra-cotta, very dark
ϓ	433	358	5471	Brown, medium
Z	816	1005	3021	Garnet
✦	834	874	2874	Golden Olive, very light
A	975	355	5356	Golden Brown, dark
B	3024	397	8397	Brown-gray, very light
◎	758	882	2337	Terra-cotta, very light
●	827	160	7159	Blue, very light
□	904	258	6258	Parrot Green, very dark
■	989	242	6266	Forest Green
▤	988	243	6258	Forest Green, medium
★	987	244	6258	Forest Green, dark
○	809	130	7021	Delft
▲	937	268	6268	Avocado Green, medium
▮	208	110	4301	Lavender, very dark

Summer Landscape sampler pictured on page 42.

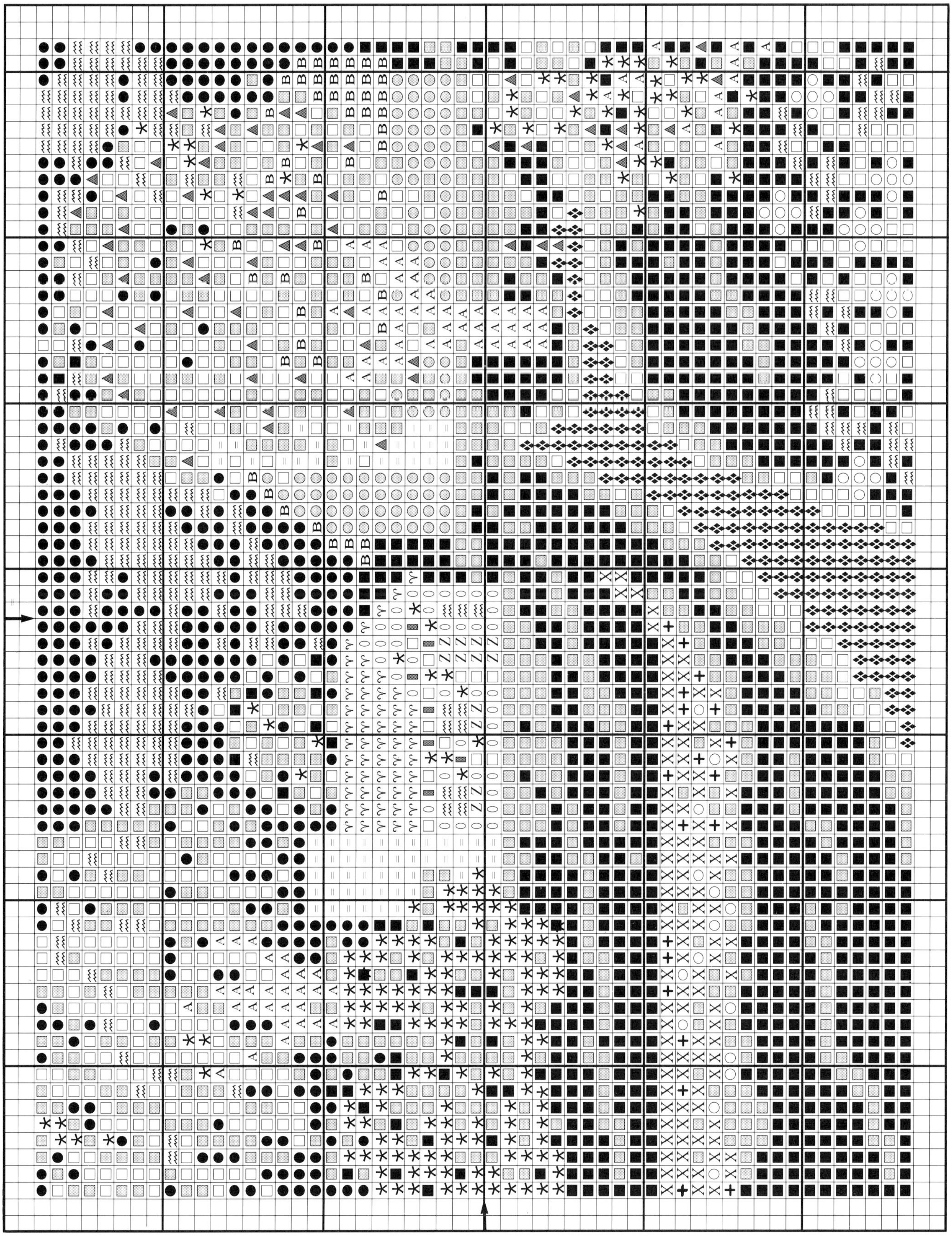

Quilt Design Pillows

These motifs were inspired by the hand-quilted scrolls and wreaths of traditional American quilts. Snow white stitches call to mind beautiful white work. Quick and easy to stitch, these designs are excellent choices for a beginner, and they're fun, fast projects for the experienced stitcher. Select fabric, floss, and edging/backing fabric to suit your taste and decor. This simple design is the perfect opportunity to experiment with a variegated or hand-dyed thread, or with beads.

■ ■ ■ ■ ■ ■ ■ ■ ■

SIZES: 14 inches diameter (35.5cm) for round pillow, 16 × 16 inches (40.5 × 40.5cm) for square pillow

FABRIC: Stitched on 14-count colonial blue Aida

STITCH COUNT: 168 × 168

YOU WILL NEED:

- 14-count colonial blue Aida no. 3706-522 from Wichelt, cut 20 inches (51cm) square
- Six-strand embroidery floss as listed in color key
- Tapestry needle size 24
- Stuffing or pillow forms: 14 inches (35.5cm) round; 16 inches (40.5cm) square
- Polyester fiberfill for stuffing corded edge
- Matching thread
- 1 yard (91.4cm) 60-inch (1.5m)-wide fabric for pillow back and corded edgings
- Seam sealant such as Fray Check

OPTIONS:

Fabric	Design Size
Aida 11	15¼ × 15¼ inches (38.5 × 38.5cm)
Aida 16	10½ × 10½ inches (26.5 × 26.5cm)
Aida 18	9⅜ × 9⅜ inches (24 × 24cm)
Hardanger 22	15¼ × 15¼ inches (38.5 × 38.5cm)

INSTRUCTIONS: Cross-stitch using three strands of floss and work over one thread of fabric.

PILLOW ASSEMBLY: Using the embroidered design area as a guide, and leaving at least 1½ inches (4cm) unworked fabric all around, mark the top edges of the pillow. Measure out evenly from the center to ensure that the design is centered.

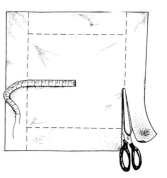

Pillows begin with a 15-inch (38cm) circle and a 16-inch (40.5cm) square, as shown. Use a dessert plate to mark rounded corners on the squares.

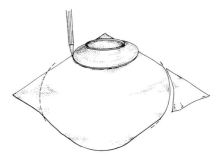

Cut a contrasting fabric back to same size as pillow front.

Corded Edging: From remaining fabric, cut 4½-inch (11.5cm) -wide strips on the diagonal to a length totaling 1 inch (2.5cm) more than the circumference of the pillow back.

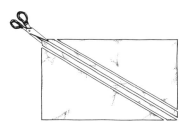

Cut ends on a 45° angle.

With right sides facing, stitch the ends together to form a ring.

Fold the fabric ring lengthwise in half, with wrong sides facing. Place edges under the presser foot of your sewing machine and machine baste ⅜ inch (1cm) from raw edges; stop every 6 inches (15cm) or so to stuff the area you have stitched. Stuff softly: use just enough to round out the tube.

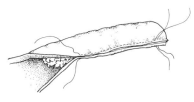

Divide corded edging into quarters and mark midpoints on pillow front. Pin stuffed edging to pillow front, with raw edges together.

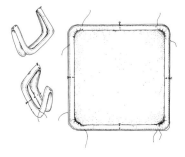

Baste around, ⅝ inch (1.5cm) from edge. Place on pillow back,

Quilt Design Pillows

right sides facing, and stitch around on previous stitching line, leaving an opening for turning. Clip into seam allowances along curves. Turn pillow right side out, insert form or stuffing, and slip stitch opening closed.

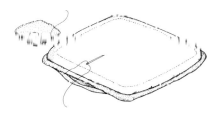

The following are variations of the Quilt Design Pillows shown on page 48.

Beaded Pillow

YOU WILL NEED:

- 28-count no. 3234 pastel linen in apricot, no. 041 from Zweigart, cut 20 inches (51cm) square
- Six-strand embroidery floss as listed in color key, one skein each
- 11 packages Mill Hill Glass Beads no. 03028
- Tapestry needle size 26
- 16-inch (40.5cm) square pillow form or stuffing
- Polyester fiberfill for stuffing
- Matching thread
- 14-inch (35.5cm) square piece of fabric for pillow back
- Seam sealant such as Fray Check
- 5 skeins Caron Watercolors thread no. 082 Gobi Sand
- One ½-inch (1.5cm) shank-type, old-style button

INSTRUCTIONS: Make cross-stitches using two strands of floss, one bead per stitch, and work over one thread of fabric. Assemble as above, omitting the corded edge.

To Make a Twisted Cord. Untwist one skein of hand-painted thread. Fold in half. Repeat for all but one of the remaining skeins; set that aside for a tassel. Group folded skeins together. Hold one end and have a friend hold the other. Twist simultaneously, in opposite directions. Continue until twist is very tight. Holding the twist so it doesn't collapse, give your end to your friend. Have your friend hold both ends in one hand, while you hold the middle. Let go, and slide your hands from ends to middle. The thread will twist up on itself and hold the twist. Knot the ends to secure.

Hand stitch the twisted cord to the edge of the pillow. Trim away the excess and reserve for the tassel. Overlap the raw edges and tuck them neatly under the twist.

To Make the Tassel: Untwist the remaining skein of hand-painted floss. Wind over a 5-inch (13cm) wide piece of cardboard securely. Tie along one edge with a scrap of the thread, leaving long tails. Cut along opposite cardboard edge and remove cardboard. About 1 inch (2.5cm) below the tie, wrap thread remaining from the twisted cord tightly around the tassel. Secure with sewing thread. Trim the bottom edge of the tassel evenly. Sew the button to the pillow as shown. Tie the thread tails from the tassel around the button. Trim the threads.

Red Pillow

Follow the instructions for the blue round pillow. Substitute 14-count royal classic rich cranberry evenweave from Charles Craft, cut 20 inches (51cm) square, and Encore no. E64 thread from Rainbow Gallery, using one strand.

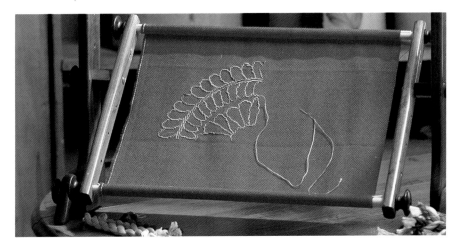

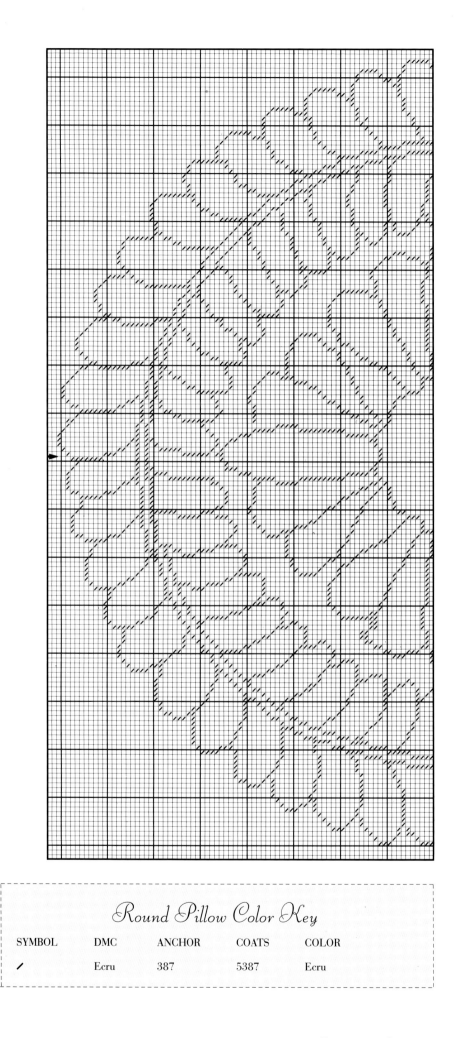

Round Pillow Color Key

SYMBOL	DMC	ANCHOR	COATS	COLOR
╱	Ecru	387	5387	Ecru

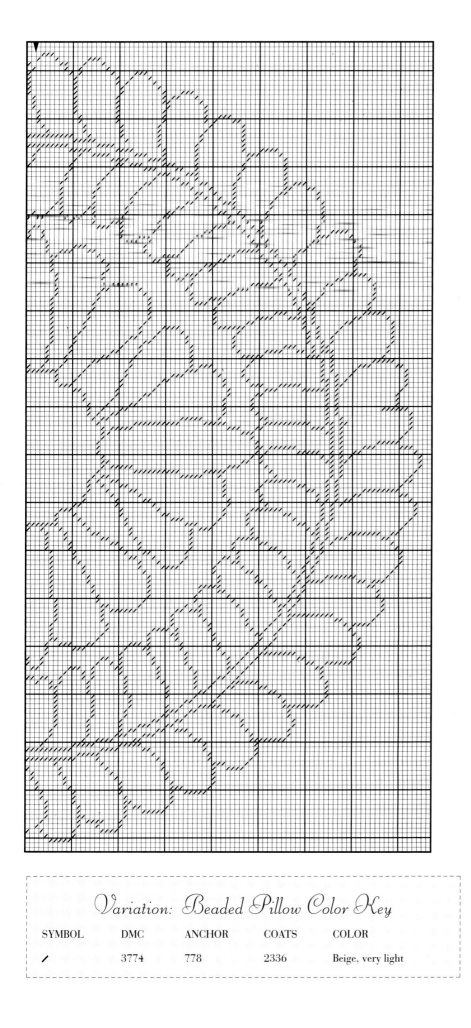

Variation: Beaded Pillow Color Key

SYMBOL	DMC	ANCHOR	COATS	COLOR
∕	3774	778	2336	Beige, very light

Round Pillow

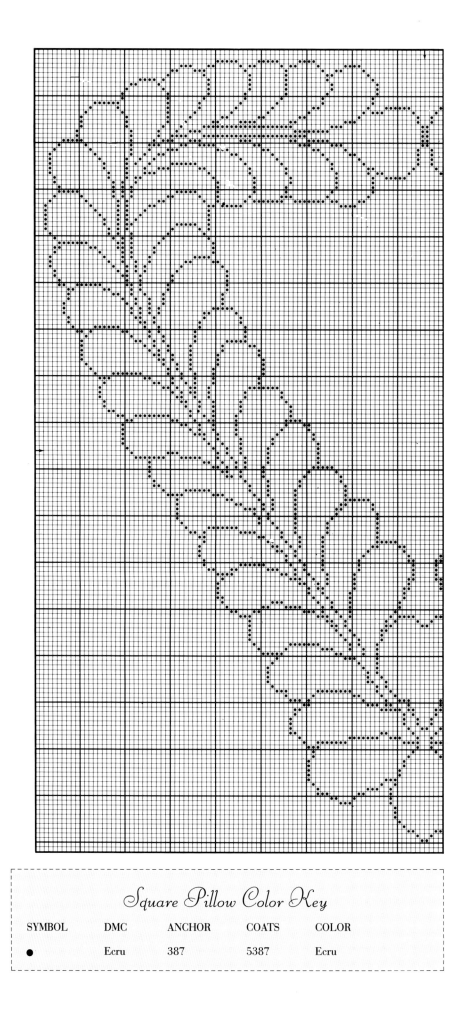

Square Pillow Color Key

SYMBOL	DMC	ANCHOR	COATS	COLOR
●	Ecru	387	5387	Ecru

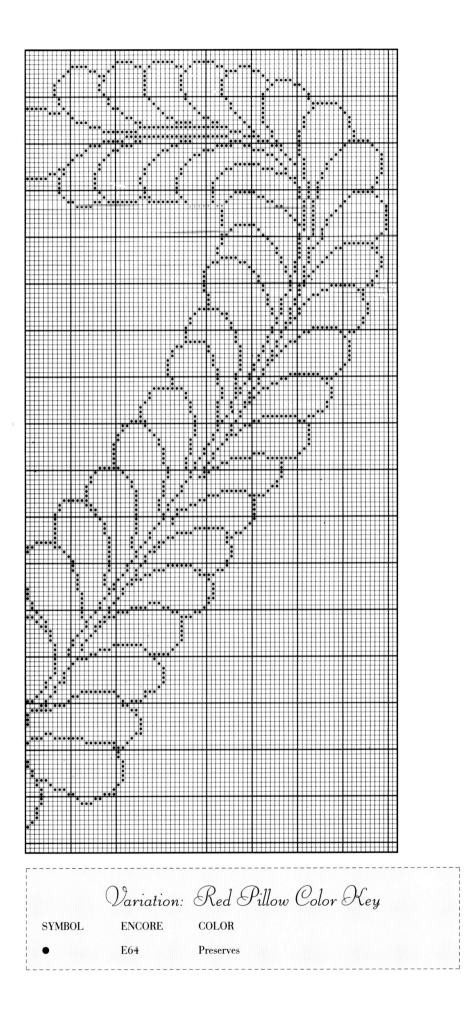

Square Pillow

Kitty in a Window

A tabby cat sharing the sill with a houseplant is entranced by those denizens of summer, robin redbreasts.

■ ■ ■ ■ ■ ■ ■ ■ ■ ■

SIZE: Framed, 11 × 12 inches (28 × 30.5cm); design area of embroidery (not including curtains), 5 × 7 inches (13 × 18cm)

FABRIC: Background stitched on 28-count light blue Brittney; foreground (kitty) stitched on 14-count white Aida

STITCH COUNT: 70 × 98; background: 70 × 61; foreground: 70 × 60

YOU WILL NEED:

■ 28-count light blue Brittney no. 3270 light blue no. 501 from Zweigart, cut 11 × 13 inches (28 × 33cm)

■ 14-count white Aida from Charles Craft, cut 11 inches (28cm) square

■ Six-strand embroidery floss as listed in color key, one skein each

■ Fabric stiffener

■ Tapestry needles sizes 24 and 26

FOR FRAMING:

■ 1 yard (91.4cm) scallop-edge white eyelet fabric

■ White sewing thread

■ ¼ × 10-inch (6mm × 25.5cm) wood or plastic dowel for curtain rod

■ 4 clear shank ³⁄₈-inch (1cm) buttons

■ Epoxy or hot glue

INSTRUCTIONS: Cross-stitch the foreground using two strands of floss. Apply fabric stiffener as instructed on the bottle. When dry, cut out just beyond the stitching.

Stitch the background using half and full cross-stitches as indicated on the chart. Make cross-stitches for the robins' eyes, then make French knots on top.

FRAMING OPTION: Lay the kitty on top of the background so the top edge of the kitty lines up with the bottom edge of the background design. Glue buttons between foreground and background near top edge.

TO MAKE THE CURTAINS: Cut two 10-inch (25.5cm) square panels, two 1½ × 5-inch (4 × 13cm) tiebacks, and one 4 × 24-inch (10 × 61cm) valance with scallops along one long edge. Finish raw edges. Make fabric tubes from tiebacks. Turn straight long edge of valance 1 inch (2.5cm) to wrong side and machine stitch ½ inch (1.5cm) and ⅞ inch (2cm) from fold, for casing. Gather valance onto wood or plastic dowel. Glue panels, held halfway with tieback, to sides of background, valance across the top. Insert in a frame with a 7½ × 9-inch (19 × 23cm) opening.

Kitty in a Window Color Key

SYMBOL	DMC	ANCHOR	COATS	COLOR
FOREGROUND: Cross-stitch with 2 strands:				
X	433	358	5471	Brown, medium
◉	435	1046	5371	Brown, very light
●	437	362	5942	Tan, light
⌘	319	218	6246	Pistachio Green, very dark
■	367	217	6018	Pistachio Green, dark
>	320	215	6017	Pistachio Green, medium
✄	368	214	6016	Pistachio Green, light
▦	355	1014	2339	Terra-cotta, dark
○	356	5975	2338	Terra-cotta, medium
=	3778	1013	2338	Terra-cotta, light
＼	758	882	2337	Terra-cotta, very light
Backstitch with 1 strand:				
—	938	381	5381	Coffee Brown, ultra dark (kitty)
—	890	218	6021	Pistachio Green, ultra dark (ivy)
BACKGROUND: Cross-stitch with 2 strands:				
■	783	307	5307	Topaz, medium
Cross-stitch with 1 strand:				
○	White	2	1001	White
＼	727	293	2289	Topaz, very light
X	806	169	7169	Peacock Blue, dark
<	3766	167	7168	Peacock Blue, light
▢	921	1003	—	Copper
✠	3787	—	—	Brown-gray, dark
❖	937	268	6268	Avocado Green, medium
⌘	469	267	6261	Avocado Green
French knots with 1 strand:				
◢	3021	905	5395	Brown-gray, very dark

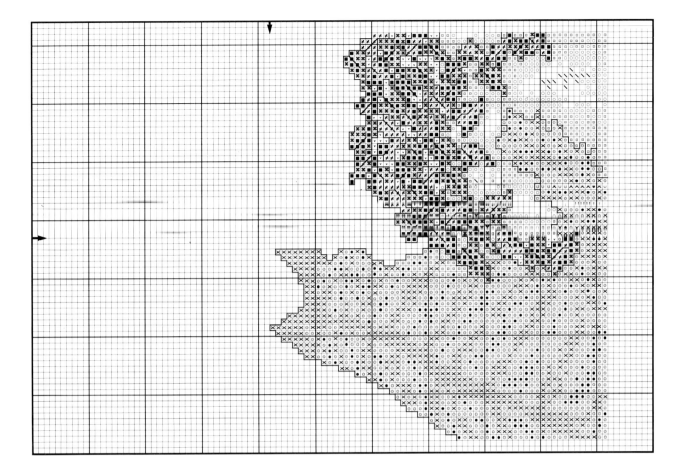

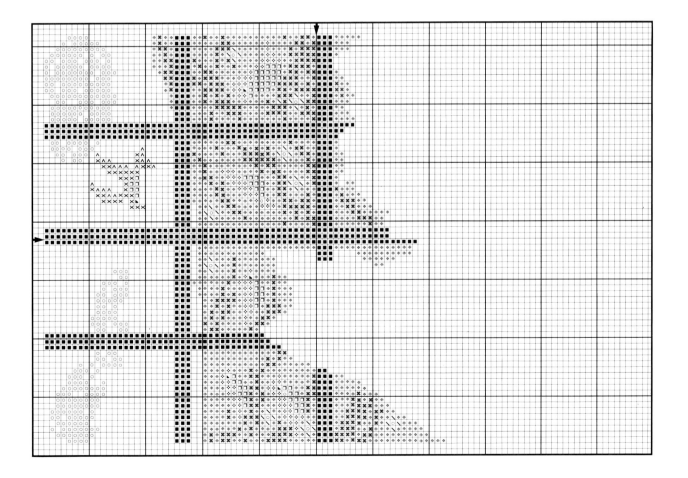

Kitty in a Window

Victorian Porch

Hand-painted ceramic buttons add color and whimsy to this easily stitched project.
Fancy matting takes it a step further.

■ ■ ■ ■ ■ ■ ■ ■ ■ ■ ■

SIZE: Framed, 13 × 16 inches (33 × 40.5cm); design area, 4½ × 6⅜ inches (11.5 × 16cm)

FABRIC: Stitched on 14-count gray Yorkshire Aida

STITCH COUNT: 63 × 89

YOU WILL NEED:
- 14-count Yorkshire Aida no. 3222 pewter no. 539 from Zweigart, cut 11 × 13 inches (28 × 33cm)
- Six-strand embroidery floss as listed in color key, one skein each
- Tapestry needle size 24
- Buttons from Mill Hill: three birdhouses, one pot of geraniums, one bluebird
- 17 white Mill Hill glass seed beads no. 00479
- Small black ball button for doorknob

OPTIONS:

Fabric	Design Size
Aida 16	4 × 5½ inches (10 × 14cm)
Aida 18	3½ × 5 inches (9 × 13cm)
Linen 28	4½ × 6⅜ inches (11.5 × 16cm)

INSTRUCTIONS: Cross-stitch over one thread using three strands of floss. For the beads at the bottom edge of the door window shade, pass the needle through each bead on both stitches of the cross-stitch. This way the beads will stand straight up and down. Stitch the buttons in place, referring to the photograph for suggested placement.

FRAMING OPTION: Trace the half pattern for gingerbread molding on tracing paper folded in half, with long dash lines along fold. Trace right half to complete pattern. Place complete pattern on illustration board or poster board and go over lines to impress them. Use a craft knife to cut bottom curve and triangular cutouts only. Insert within picture mat cut to gable shape for top edge.

As an alternative, purchase appropriate dollhouse molding.

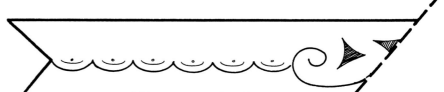

This pattern reduced to 85%

Color Key

SYMBOL	DMC	ANCHOR	COATS	COLOR
Cross-stitch with 3 strands:				
A	434	310	5000	Brown, light
●	801	359	5472	Coffee Brown, dark
/	436	1045	5943	Tan
□	White	2	1001	White
■	414	235	8513	Steel Gray, dark
=	3325	129	7976	Baby Blue, light
#	762	234	8510	Pearl Gray, very light
8				White Mill Hill glass seed beads

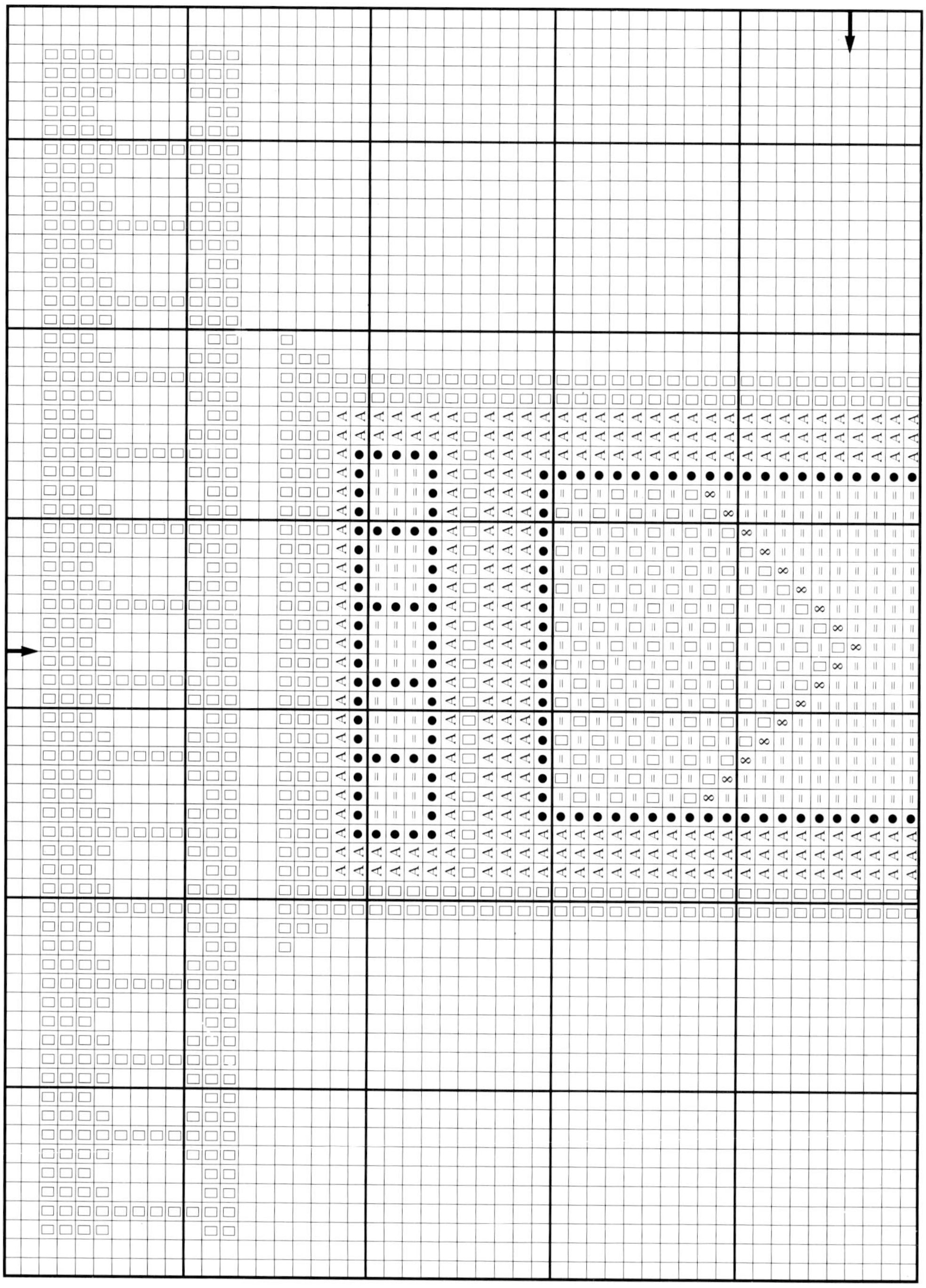

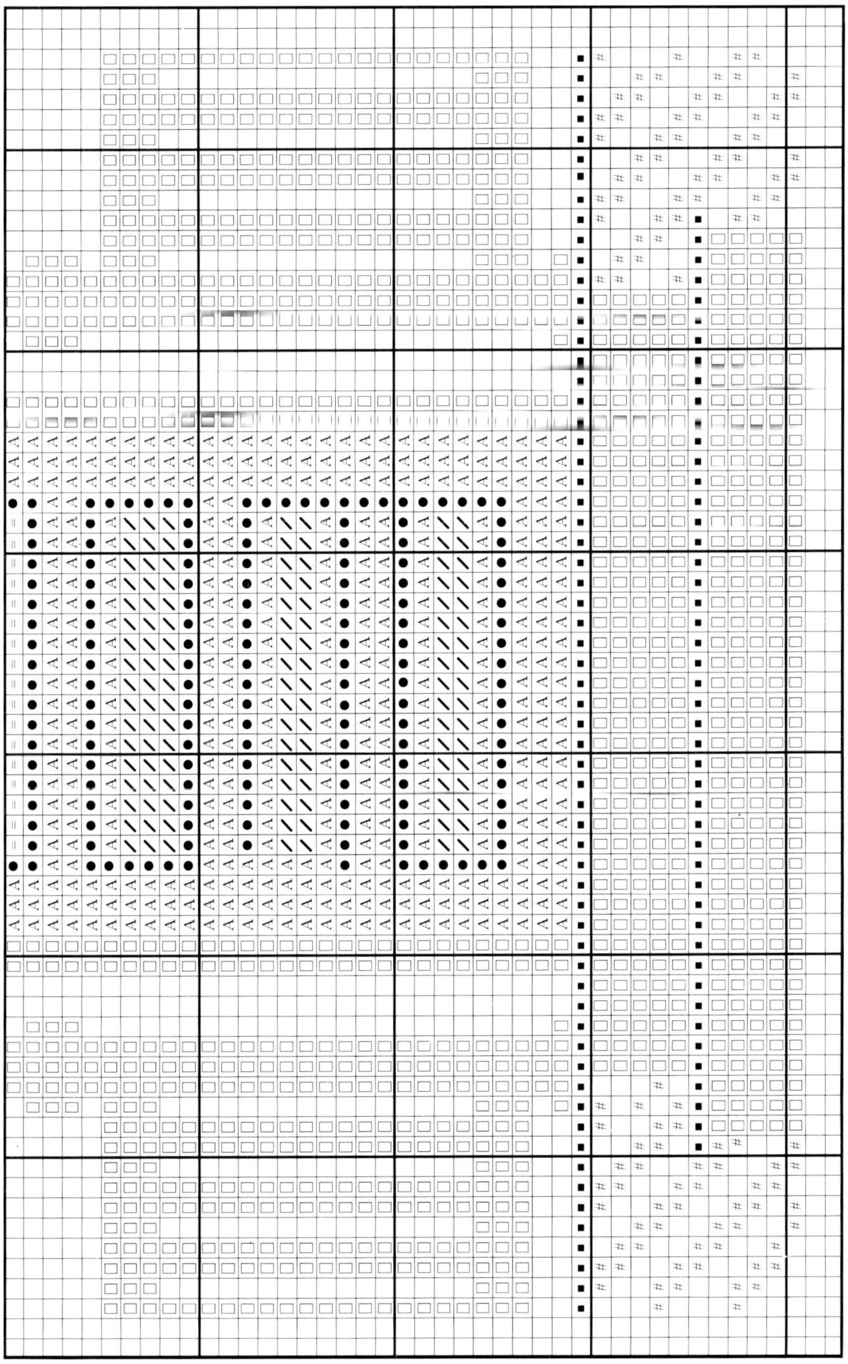

Berry Sampler

Hand-painted threads stitch up into a luscious plaque celebrating golden summer days.

■ ■ ■ ■ ■ ■ ■ ■ ■ ■

SIZE: Framed, 16½ × 21⅞ inches (42 × 55.5cm); design area, 8½ × 13½ inches (21.5 × 34.5cm)

FABRIC: Stitched on 28-count yellow Jubilee linen

STITCH COUNT: 120 × 190

YOU WILL NEED:

▪ 28-count Jubilee linen no. 3232 in yellow no. 281 from Zweigart, cut 15 × 20 inches (38 × 51cm)

▪ Six-strand embroidery floss as listed in color key, one skein each

▪ Caron Wildflowers thread (CW) as listed in the color key, one skein each

▪ DMC variegated (DMC V) thread as listed in the color key, one skein each

▪ Tapestry needle size 26

OPTIONS:

Fabric	Design Size
Linen 25	9½ × 15¼ inches (24 × 38.5cm)
Linen 30	8 × 12⅝ inches (20.5 × 32cm)

INSTRUCTIONS: Cross-stitch using two strands of floss. Referring to the alphabet on the sampler, cross-stitch initials in the area shaded gray on chart. Make three-quarter cross-stitches at small versions of symbols. Backstitch with one strand. Make French knots with one strand.

Color Key

SYMBOL	DMC	DMC V	CW	COLOR
Cross-stitch with 2 strands:				
#	414			Steel Gray, dark
/	415			Pearl Gray
X			090	Ruby
●			012	Wildberries
□	Ecru			
▨		122		Green
■		124		Periwinkle Blue
^	413			Pewter Gray, dark
Backstitch with 1 strand:				
—	413			Pewter Gray, dark (urn)
—	987			Forest Green, dark (leaves)
—	301			Mahogany, medium (border and flowers and stems in border)
—	311			Navy Blue, medium (ribbons)
—			012	Wildberries (berries)
—		121		Blue (intertwined squiggles)
—			065	Emerald (top and bottom border squiggles)
French knots with 1 strand:				
●		121		Blue (intertwined squiggles and around lower-case alphabet)
●			065	Emerald (top and bottom border squiggles)
Satin stitch with 1 strand:				
=		122		Green (bricks pattern at sides of lowercase alphabet)

FRAMING OPTION: Place in a triple mat with top and bottom edges scalloped to echo contours of needlework. Frame opening is 14½ × 20 inches (37 × 51cm).

Berry Sampler

Autumn

· · · · · · · · · ·

Leaves falling on crisp breezes, fresh cider
to sip, and a crackling fire to cozy up to: no wonder
autumn is such a celebrated season.

Taking a cue from Mother Nature, I find myself
mimicking autumn's preparation for hibernation. The
sun sets early, and I look forward to longer evenings
of stitching. An abundance of foods fresh from the
harvest produces delicious fragrances from the kitchen
as I stitch. Canning and freezing will preserve these
foods for seasons to come, just as my cross-stitching
preserves my sense of nature's splendor.

In this chapter, I celebrate the harvest: A pepper
sampler features black metallic chicken wire; an Indian
corn, sunflower, and miniature pumpkin wreath
welcomes friends to your home. Baskets, a symbol of
the harvest, and quilts, which now come out to ward
off the increasing chill, are traditional motifs of the
season. And what can be more appropriate for autumn
than a quaint village, much like those in New England
so treasured by seekers of autumn foliage?

Autumn Landscape

The color palette turns to rich earth tones in the autumn rendition of our quaint scene.

■ ■ ■ ■ ■ ■ ■ ■ ■ ■

SIZE: Framed, 10½ × 9½ inches (26.5 × 24cm); design area, 5 × 3⅞ inches (13 × 10cm)

FABRIC: Stitched on 14-count white Aida over one thread

STITCH COUNT: 70 × 55

YOU WILL NEED:

- 14-count white Aida from Charles Craft, cut 11 inches (28cm) square
- Six-strand embroidery floss as listed in color key, one skein each
- Tapestry needle size 24

OPTIONS:

Fabric	Design Size
Aida 11	6⅜ × 5 inches (16 × 13cm)
Aida 16	4⅜ × 3¼ inches (11 × 8cm)
Aida 18	3⅞ × 3 inches (10 × 7.5cm)

INSTRUCTIONS: Cross-stitch using two strands of floss and work over one thread of fabric.

FRAMING OPTION: Paint oak leaves and acorns in upper left corner of outer mat. Insert in a frame with an 8¾ × 7¾-inch (22 × 19.5cm) opening, using a double mat.

Color Key

SYMBOL	DMC	ANCHOR	COATS	COLOR
Cross-stitch with 2 strands:				
~	844	1041	8501	Beaver Brown, ultra dark
▲	782	308	5308	Topaz, dark
✠	3787	—	—	Brown-gray
<	White	2	1001	White
□	3777	1015	2339	Terra-cotta, very dark
V	433	358	5471	Brown, medium
Z	816	1005	3021	Garnet
✶	834	874	2874	Golden Olive, very light
%	975	355	5356	Golden Brown, dark
B	3023	—	—	Brown-gray, light
❖	758	882	2337	Terra-cotta, very light
◉	827	160	7159	Blue, very light
X	904	258	6258	Parrot Green, very dark
#	937	268	6268	Avocado Green, medium
0	895	1044	6021	Hunter Green, very dark
■	906	256	6256	Parrot Green, medium
◆	905	257	6258	Parrot Green, dark
▧	326	59	3401	Rose, very deep
A	725	305	2294	Topaz
—	921	1003	—	Copper
▯	783	307	5307	Topaz, medium
/	721	3324	2324	Orange Spice, medium
●	445	288	2288	Lemon, light
=	444	290	2290	Lemon, dark
S	3685	1028	3089	Mauve, dark
≋	726	295	2295	Topaz, light

Autumn Landscape sampler pictured on page 66.

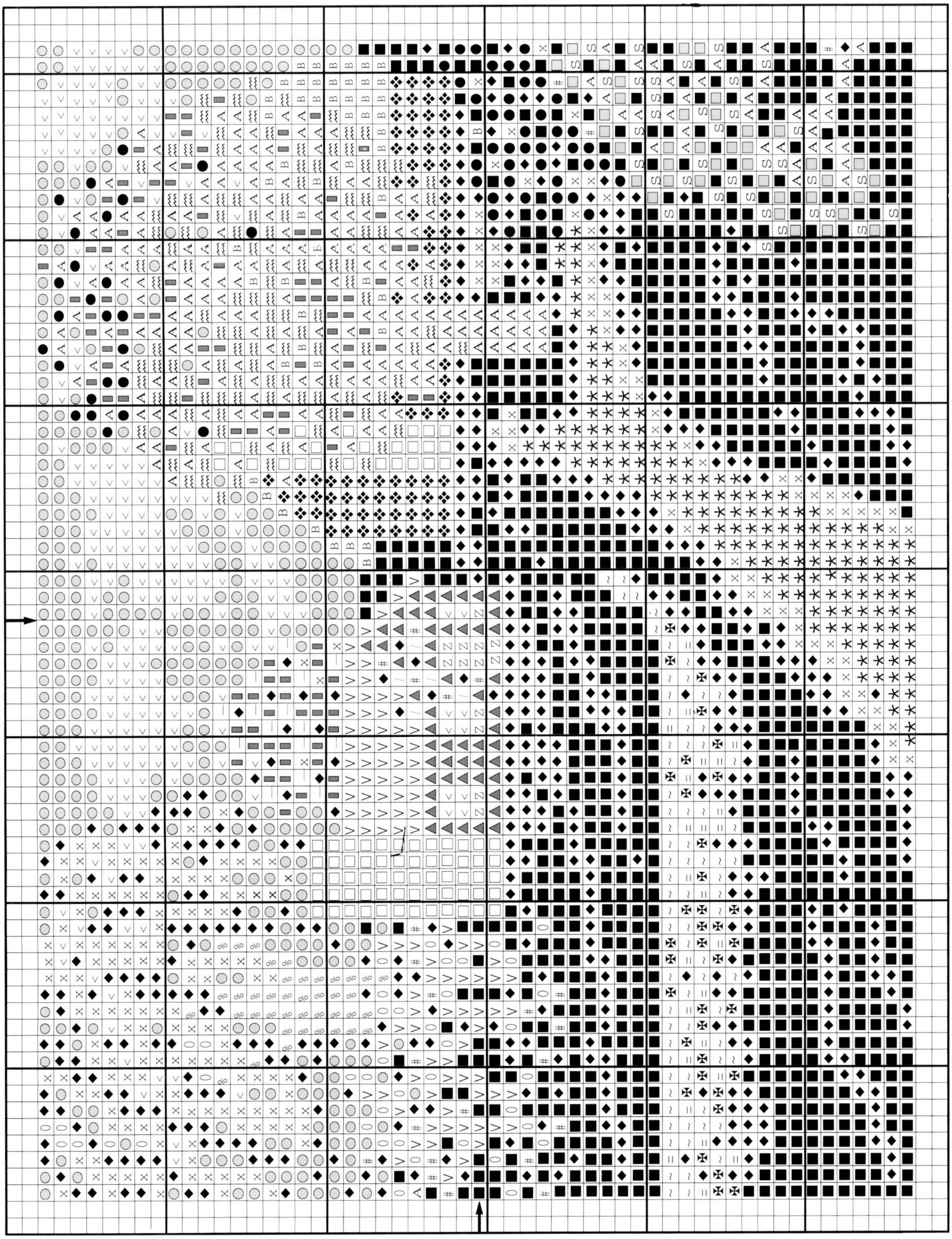

Peppers

Crunchy sweet or blazing hot, pick your favorite pepper from this home-style wall chart.

■ ■ ■ ■ ■ ■ ■ ■ ■ ■ ■

SIZE: Framed, 18 × 11½ inches (45.5 × 29cm); design area, 15 × 8⅜ inches (38 × 21cm)

FABRIC: Stitched on 14-count Linaida over one thread

STITCH COUNT: 210 × 113

YOU WILL NEED:

- 14-count Linaida from Charles Craft, cut 21 × 14 inches (53.5 × 35.5cm)
- Six-strand embroidery floss as listed in color key, one skein each
- One skein black metallic thread
- Tapestry needle size 24

OPTIONS:

Fabric	Design Size
Aida 11	19 × 10⅛ inches (48 × 25.5cm)
Aida 18	11⅝ × 6¼ inches (29.5 × 16cm)
Hardanger 22	19 × 10⅛ inches (48 × 25.5cm)
Linen 25	16⅞ × 9 inches (43 × 23cm)

Color Key

SYMBOL	DMC	ANCHOR	COATS	COLOR
Cross-stitch with 2 strands:				
●	745	300	2296	Yellow, light pale
2	3705	35	3012	Melon, dark
□	909	923	6228	Emerald Green, medium
?	725	305	2294	Topaz
=	726	295	2295	Topaz, light
B	727	293	2289	Topaz, very light
A	922	1003	3336	Copper, light
I	304	1006	3410	Christmas Red, medium
>	817	13	2335	Coral Red, very dark
#	349	13	2335	Coral, dark
h	350	11	3111	Coral, medium
▼	470	267	6010	Avocado Green, light
V	699	923	6228	Christmas Green
*	369	1043	6015	Pistachio Green, very light
:	701	227	6226	Christmas Green, light
N	910	229	6031	Emerald Green, dark
Backstitch with 1 strand:				
—	Black metallic			(wire)
—	349	13	2335	Coral, dark (lettering)

INSTRUCTIONS: Cross-stitch using two strands of floss and work over one strand of fabric. Use one strand for backstitch, working chicken-wire pattern first, then lettering.

FRAMING OPTION: Insert in a frame with a 15¾ × 9¼-inch (40 × 23.5cm) opening.

Harvest Welcome Wreath

Greet your guests with a warm sign of your hospitality.

■ ■ ■ ■ ■ ■ ■ ■ ■ ■

SIZE: Framed, 19⅜ × 16⅜ inches (49 × 41.5 cm); design area, 11 × 8¼ inches (28 × 21 cm)

FABRIC: Stitched on 11-count royal blue Aida

STITCH COUNT: 125 × 92

YOU WILL NEED:

▪ 11-count royal blue Aida no. 1007-567 dark blue from Wichelt, cut 18 × 15 inches (45.5 × 38 cm)
▪ Six-strand embroidery floss as listed in color key, one skein each
▪ Tapestry needle size 24

OPTIONS:

Fabric	Design Size
Aida 14	9 × 6½ inches (23 × 16.5 cm)
Aida 16	7¾ × 5¾ inches (19.5 × 14.5 cm)
Aida 18	7 × 5⅛ inches (18 × 13 cm)
Linen 25	10 × 7⅜ inches (25.5 × 18.5 cm)

INSTRUCTIONS: Cross-stitch using three strands of floss and work over one thread of fabric. Backstitch with one strand.

FRAMING OPTION: Use a triple mat with an inside window 12½ × 9½ inches (31.5 × 24 cm), and insert in a frame with a 17 × 14-inch (43 × 35.5 cm) opening.

Color Key

SYMBOL	DMC	ANCHOR	COATS	COLOR
Cross-stitch with 3 strands:				
○	727	293	2289	Topaz, very light
✵	726	295	2295	Topaz, light
≈	725	305	2295	Topaz
▽	921	1003	—	Copper
+	721	3324	2324	Orange Spice, medium
□	720	326	2322	Orange Spice, dark
●	722	323	2323	Orange Spice, light
⌘	472	253	6253	Avocado Green, ultra light
ɪ	471	266	6266	Avocado Green, very light
#	470	267	6010	Avocado Green, light
●	469	267	6261	Avocado Green
/	936	269	6269	Avocado Green, very dark
?	3012	844	6844	Khaki Green, medium
⊠	3011	846	6845	Khaki Green, dark
B	413	401	8514	Pewter Gray, dark
✳	3778	1013	2338	Terra Cotta, light
%	3776	1048	3336	Mahogany, light
△	3047	852	2300	Yellow-beige, light
▲	3046	887	2410	Yellow-beige, medium
S	3045	888	2412	Yellow-beige, dark
■	433	358	5471	Brown, medium
❖	535	—	8400	Ash Gray, very light
◎	938	381	5381	Coffee Brown, ultra light
■	976	1001	2308	Golden Brown, medium
✠	3371	382	5382	Black-brown
Backstitch with 1 strand:				
—	919	340	2326	Red-copper (pumpkins)
—	934	862	6270	Avocado Green, dark (leaves)
—	782	308	5308	Topaz, dark (sunflowers)
—	3011	846	6845	Khaki Green, dark (pumpkin stems)
—	3045	888	2412	Yellow-beige, dark (corn husks)

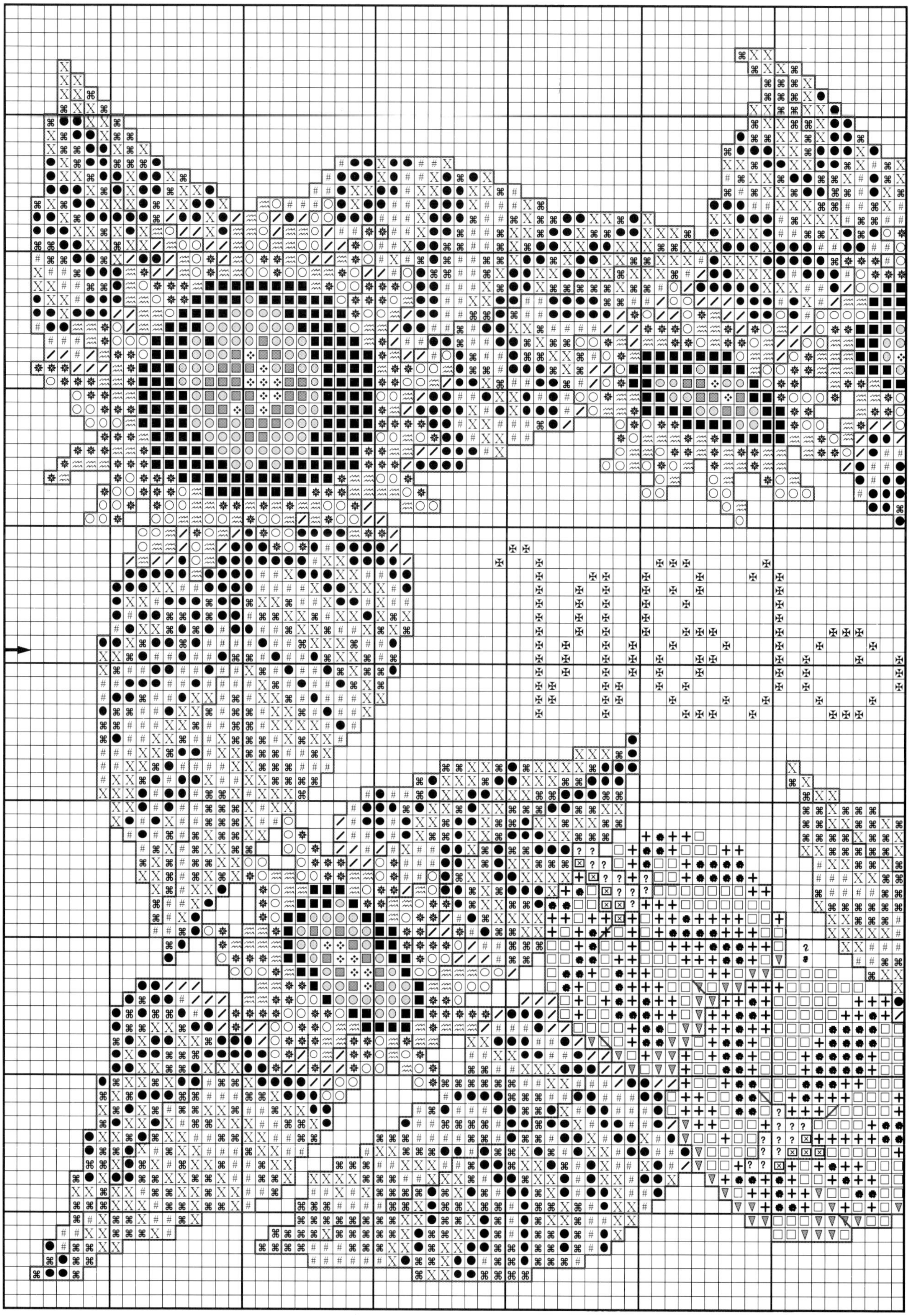

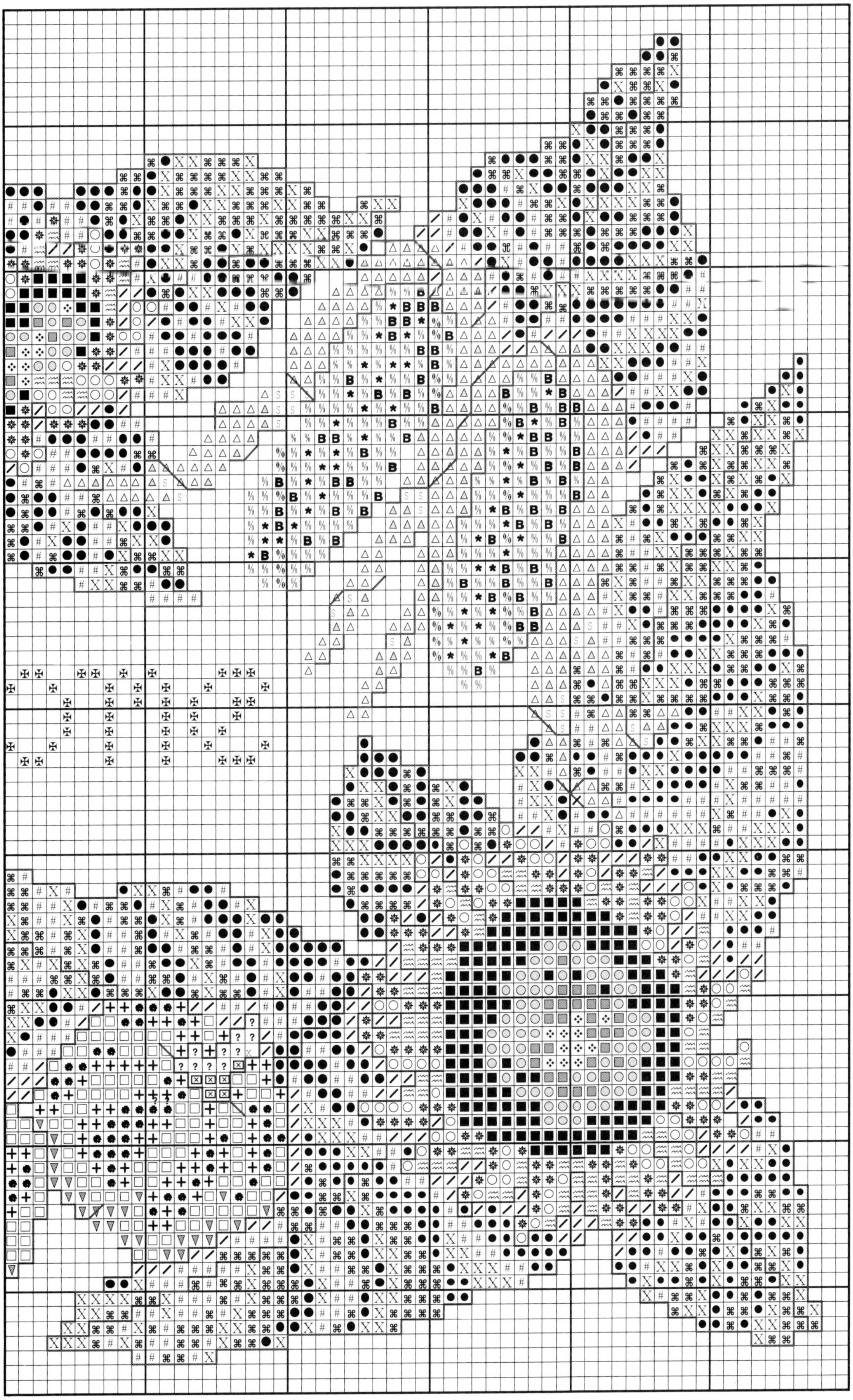

Quilt Baskets

Brighten hearts with these baskets full of cheer. Variegated floss produces soft gradations in color almost magically. For a striking, traditional Amish look, consider stitching the baskets on black background fabric.

■ ■ ■ ■ ■ ■ ■ ■ ■ ■ ■

SIZE: Framed, $11\frac{1}{4} \times 11\frac{1}{4}$ inches (28.5×28.5cm); design area, $5\frac{7}{8} \times 5\frac{7}{8}$ inches (15×15cm)

FABRIC: Stitched on 28-count cream Irish linen

DESIGN AREA: 79×79

YOU WILL NEED:

■ 28-count cream Irish linen from Charles Craft, cut 12 inches (30.5cm) square

■ Six-strand embroidery floss as listed in color key, one skein each

■ DMC variegated floss (DMC V) as indicated in color key, one skein each

OPTIONS:

Fabric	Design Size
Aida 14	$5\frac{5}{8} \times 5\frac{5}{8}$ inches (14.5×14.5cm)
Aida 18	$4\frac{3}{8} \times 4\frac{3}{8}$ inches (11×11cm)
Linen 22	$7\frac{1}{8} \times 7\frac{1}{8}$ inches (18×18cm)

INSTRUCTIONS: Wind the floss lengthwise around a yardstick, with the dark shades to one side of the center of the yardstick and the light shades to the other side.

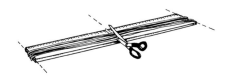

Cut the floss at both ends of the yardstick and then at the center. This will give you two shade groups: one light to medium, the other medium to dark. Do this for the green, red, purple, and blue variegated floss. Use the dark shades for the bottoms of the baskets and the light shades for the tops. Cross-stitch using two strands of floss and work over two threads of fabric. To achieve a gradual color change rather than a tweedy effect, cross each stitch as you go.

Work a four-sided stitch in black around the baskets where indicated on the chart.

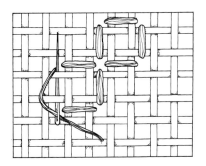

Make long straight stitches within the triangles outside the basket square using the yellow variegated thread.

Backstich around and inside the border with black floss as indicated on the chart.

FRAMING OPTION: Insert in an $11\frac{1}{4} \times 11\frac{1}{4}$-inch ($28.5 \times 28.5$cm)

frame with a double mat. Attach hanging wire across one corner so that it hangs as a diamond rather than a square.

Color Key

SYMBOL	DMC	VARIEGATED FLOSS	COLOR
Cross-stitch with 2 strands over 2 threads:			
■	114		Green, light to medium
&	114		Green, medium to dark
B	52		Purple, light to medium
∧	52		Purple, medium to dark
□	107		Red, light to medium
x	107		Red, medium to dark
#	113		Blue, light to medium
●	113		Blue, medium to dark
Long stitch with 2 strands over 6 threads:			
≡	90		Yellow
Four-sided stitch with 1 strand:			
⊐⊏	310		Black
Backstitch with 1 strand:			
—	310		Black

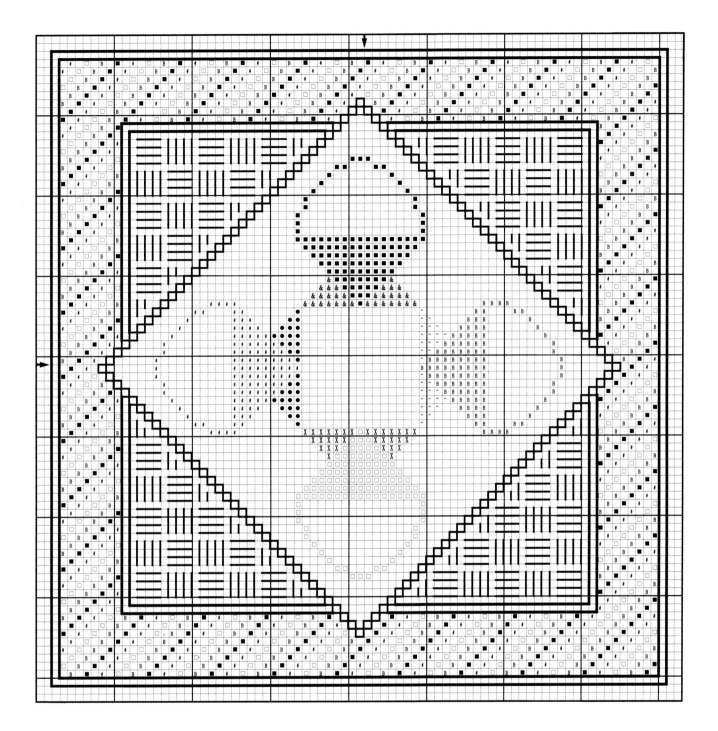

Village Sampler

Variegated, hand-dyed, and Flower threads bring painterly charm to this design.
A border grid of pulled stitches provides a puckered texture perfect for a pillow;
use a running backstitch for a framed piece.

SIZE: Pillow and design area, 14³⁄₄ × 11⁵⁄₈ inches (37.5 × 29.5cm)

FABRIC: Stitched on 26-count hickory Heatherfield

STITCH COUNT: 192 × 152

YOU WILL NEED:

- 26-count hickory Heatherfield no. 9024-16 from Wichelt, cut 21 × 18 inches (53.5 × 45.5cm)
- Caron Wildflowers (CW) threads as indicated in color key, six skeins Holiday for outer border, one skein each other threads
- DMC Flower Thread, as indicated in color key
- Tapestry needle size 26
- ½ yard (45.5cm) hunter green pinwale corduroy
- Matching sewing thread
- ¼-inch (6mm) -wide cotton cord
- Polyester fiberfill for stuffing

OPTIONS:

Fabric	Design Size
Aida 14	13⁵⁄₈ × 10⁷⁄₈ inches (13.5 × 27.5cm)
Aida 18	10⁵⁄₈ × 8³⁄₈ inches (27 × 21cm)
Linen 25	15³⁄₈ × 12¼ inches (39 × 31cm)

INSTRUCTIONS: Stitch over two threads of fabric. Where symbols have been reduced in size, make quarter cross-stitches. Make French knots for the apples and lilacs with one strand of thread. Stitch the sky and grass using half crosses. Make lazy daisy stitches in the inner border as shown.

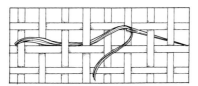

For the outer border, use a backstitch or a running backstitch (shown below).

Pulled a bit tight, the backstitch will cause the fabric to pucker, as pictured on the pillow. The running backstitch, if not tightened as it is stitched, will allow the fabric to lie flat, a better treatment for a framed version. Following the alphabet and numbers on the chart, stitch your initials and the date in the space left on the chart.

PILLOW ASSEMBLY: Trim needlework to ½ inch (1.5cm) beyond stitching all around. From corduroy, cut a same-size rectangle for pillow back. For piping, cut remaining fabric into 1½-inch (4cm) -wide strips on the bias. Piece as necessary to total 53 inches (1.3m). Fold strip around cotton cord. Use zipper foot attachment to stitch as close as possible to cord.

Pin piping around pillow front. Baste in place along stitching of piping. Pin pillow front on pillow back, right sides facing. Use zipper foot attachment to sew slightly to inside of basting stitches; leave a 5-inch (13cm) opening on bottom edge. Clip curves and turn to right side. Stuff plumply and slip stitch

Color Key

SYMBOL	DMC FLOWER THREAD	CW	COLOR
Cross-stitch with 1 strand over 2 threads:			
▽	2743		Yellow
▨	2436		Tan
❖	2898		Brown
#	2354		Brick
■	2310		Black
>	2319		Green
△	2890		Dark Green
✸	2322		Country Blue
0	White		White
X		025	Holiday
Half cross-stitches with 1 strand:			
/		065	Emerald
∴		133	Delphinium
French knots with 1 strand:			
●	2321		Red (apples)
●	2394		Purple (lilacs)
Lazy daisy stitch with 1 strand:			
⟋	2321		Red
⟋	2322		Blue
⟋		065	Emerald
Backstitch with 1 strand:			
—		133	Delphinium (lower case alphabet)
—	2898		Brown (white house: roof, windows, door; yellow house: windows, shutters, door; meeting-house: windows, doors; vine of inner border)
			White (white house, birdhouse, church)
—	2743		Yellow (yellow house, outhouse)
—	2890		Dark Green (outhouse roofs, doors; double outlines of inner border)
—	2310		Black (yellow house roof; church door, windows, and roof; meeting-house roof; birdhouse pole)
—	2354		Brick (white house, yellow house, and meetinghouse chimneys)
—	2825		Medium Blue (birds)
Running backstitch with 1 strand:			
＼		025	Holiday (6 skeins)

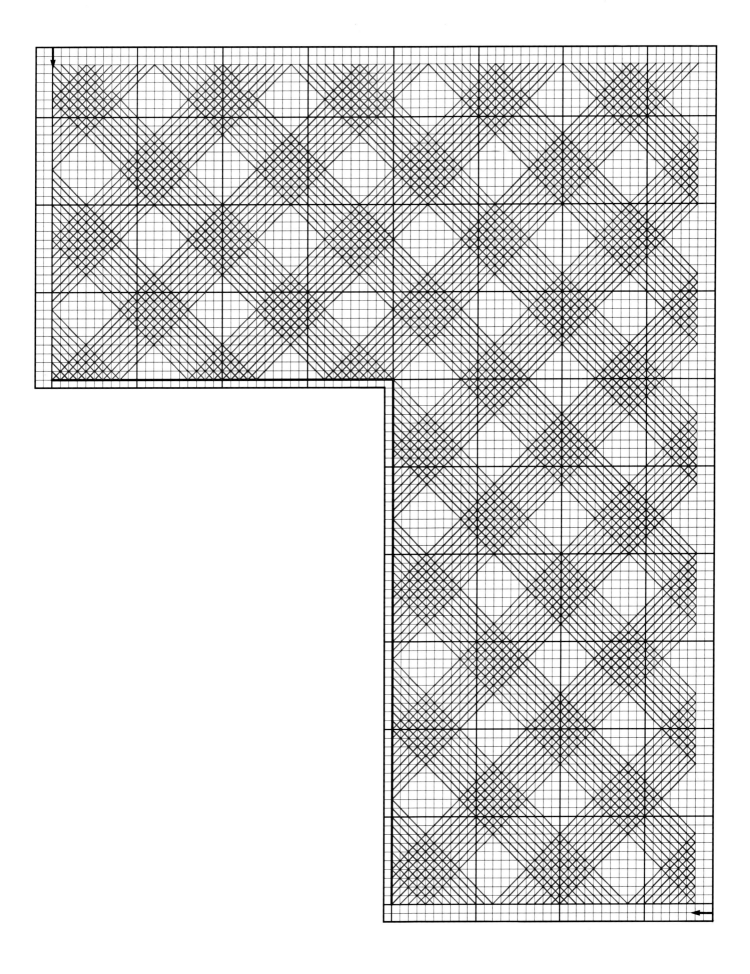

Border for Village Sampler

abcdefghyklmr

Winter

. . . .

The joy of winter stems not only from its tranquil
beauty, but also from the many opportunities for
bringing together family and friends. What better way
to savor these good times than to stitch them!
This chapter offers something for everyone. Stitch the
super-easy Christmas Wreath adorned with ornaments
borrowed from a real miniature tree, or try the
striking white-on-white Snowflake Sampler
featuring beautiful new stitches.
Whether you make them as gifts or to hang on your
own walls, these reminders of winter will bring warm
memories year after year.

Winter Landscape

Snuggled in a blanket of newly fallen snow, our log cabin casts a welcoming glow from its windows. If you have stitched all four seasons, consider framing them separately and hanging them as a group or matting them together in one frame.

▪ ▪ ▪ ▪ ▪ ▪ ▪ ▪ ▪ ▪

SIZE: Framed, $10\frac{1}{2} \times 9\frac{1}{2}$ inches (26.5 × 24cm); design area, $5 \times 3\frac{7}{8}$ inches (13 × 10cm)

FABRIC: Stitched on 14-count white Aida

STITCH COUNT: 70×55

YOU WILL NEED:

▪ 14-count white Aida, cut 11 inches (28cm) square

▪ Six-strand embroidery floss as listed in color key, one skein each

▪ Tapestry needle size 24

OPTIONS:

Fabric	Design Size
Aida 11	$6\frac{3}{8} \times 5$ inches (16 × 13cm)
Aida 16	$4\frac{3}{8} \times 3\frac{1}{4}$ inches (11 × 8cm)
Aida 18	$3\frac{7}{8} \times 2\frac{3}{4}$ inches (10 × 7cm)

INSTRUCTIONS: Cross-stitch using two strands of floss and work over one thread of fabric.

FRAMING OPTION: Paint several snowflakes in upper right corner. Insert in a frame with an $8\frac{3}{4} \times 7\frac{3}{4}$-inch (22 × 19.5cm) opening, using a double mat.

Color Key

SYMBOL	DMC	ANCHOR	COATS	COLOR
Cross-stitch with 2 strands:				
I	844	1041	8501	Beaver Brown, ultra dark
⬤	782	308	5308	Topaz, dark
●	3787	—	—	Brown-gray
○	White	2	1001	White
◎	762	234	8510	Pearl Gray, very light
▼	3777	1015	2339	Terra-cotta, very dark
▢	433	358	5471	Brown, medium
z	816	1005	3021	Garnet
△	822	390	5933	Beige-gray, light
◆	834	874	2874	Golden Olive, very light
❖	975	355	5356	Golden Brown, dark
▽	3024	397	8397	Brown-gray, very light
⌘	758	882	2337	Terra-cotta, very light
╱	827	160	7159	Blue, very light
c	743	302	2294	Yellow, medium
≈	725	305	2294	Topaz
✳	904	258	6258	Parrot Green, very dark
■	906	256	6256	Parrot Green, medium
✕	783	307	5307	Topaz, medium

Winter Landscape sampler pictured on page 88.

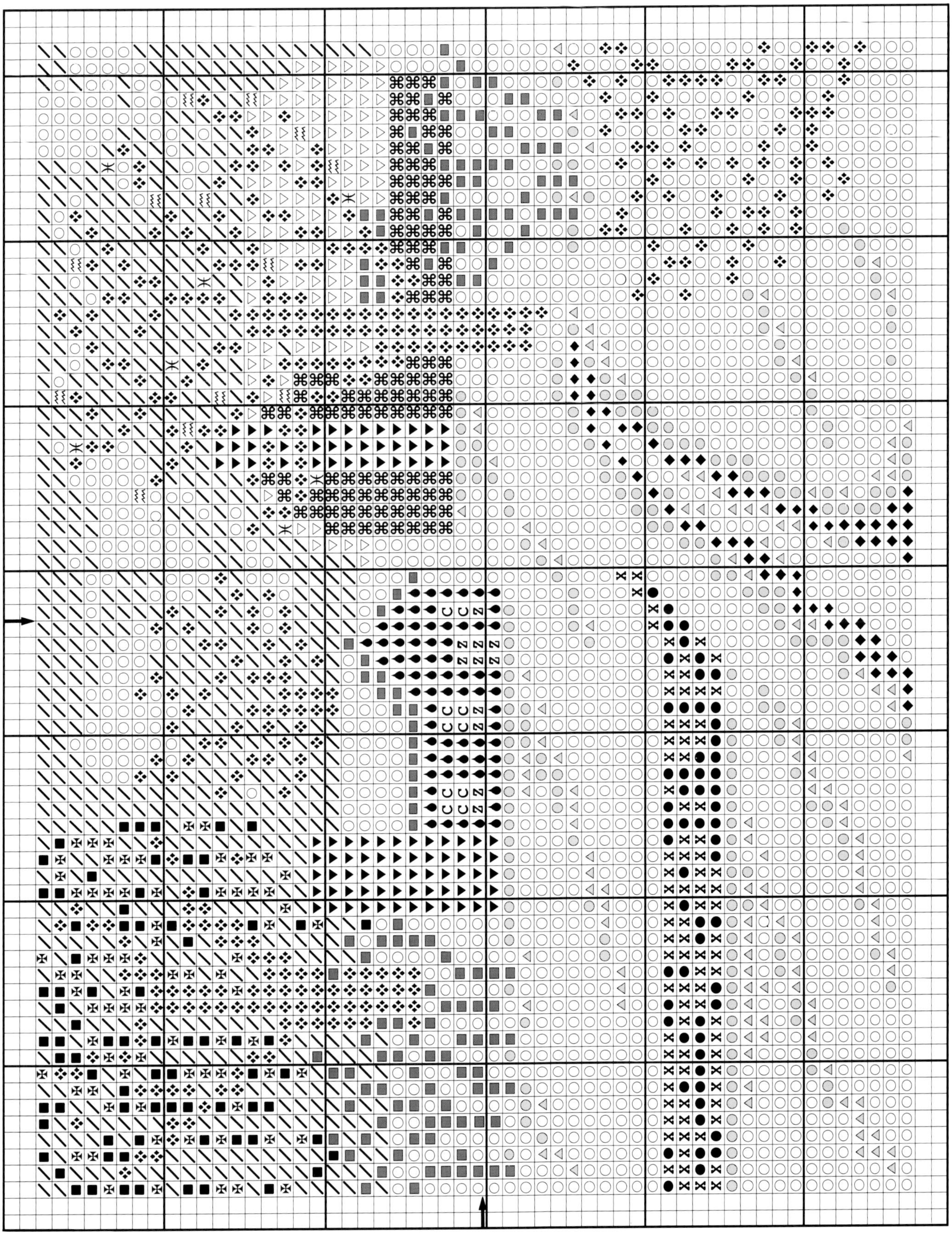

Christmas Wreath

Visit your favorite Christmas store to collect miniature Christmas ornaments for decorating this festive wreath.

■ ■ ■ ■ ■ ■ ■ ■ ■ ■

SIZE: Framed, 19½ × 20 inches (49.5 × 51cm); design area, 11½ × 11½ inches (29 × 29cm)

FABRIC: Stitched on 14-count rich cranberry plaid

STITCH COUNT: 158 × 161

YOU WILL NEED:

- 14-count rich cranberry Christmas plaid fabric from Charles Craft, cut 20 inches (51cm) square
- Six-strand embroidery floss as listed in color key, one skein each unless otherwise indicated
- Tapestry needle size 24
- 20 miniature decorations, including gift packages, ball ornaments, snowflakes, and small figures

OPTIONS:

Fabric	Design Size
Aida 11	6⅜ × 5 inches (16 × 13cm)
Aida 18	3⅞ × 2¾ inches (10 × 7cm)
Linen 25	12⅞ × 12¾ inches (32.5 × 32.5cm)

Color Key

SYMBOL	DMC	ANCHOR	COATS	COLOR
Cross-stitch with 2 strands:				
□	500	683	6880	Blue-green, very dark
■	561	212	6211	Jade, very dark
▣	562	210	6213	Jade, medium
●	563	208	6210	Jade, light
○	815	43	3000	Garnet, medium
◎	321	9046	3500	Christmas Red
'	745	300	2296	Yellow, pale
Straight stitch with 2 strands:				
▬▬▬	3782	899	5388	Mocha Brown, light (pine stems)
(Optional) Backstitch with 1 strand:				
	310	403	8403	Black (berries)

INSTRUCTIONS: Cross-stitch using two strands of floss and work over one thread of fabric. Tack miniature Chrismas tree ornaments to the wreath.

FRAMING OPTIONS: Insert in frame with a 17¼ × 17¾-inch (44 × 45cm) opening. Use a double or triple mat.

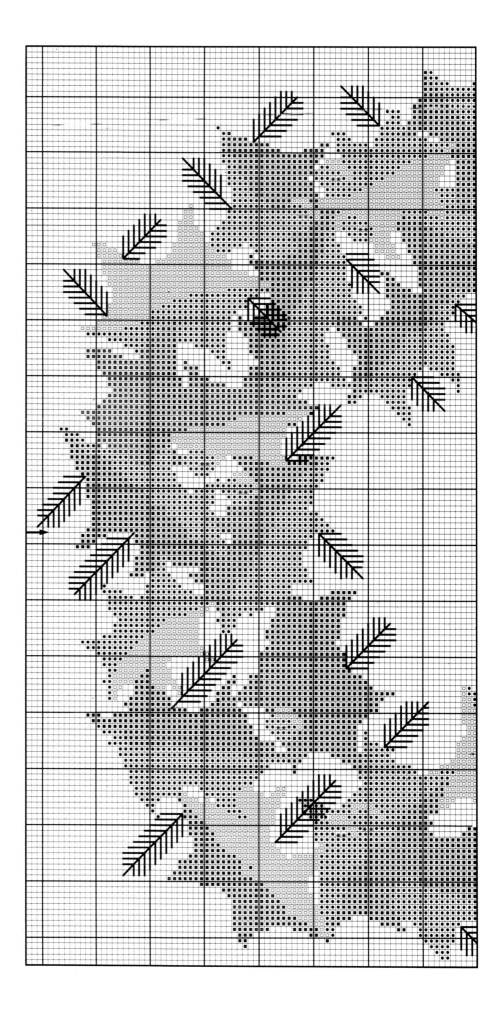

Christmas Wreath

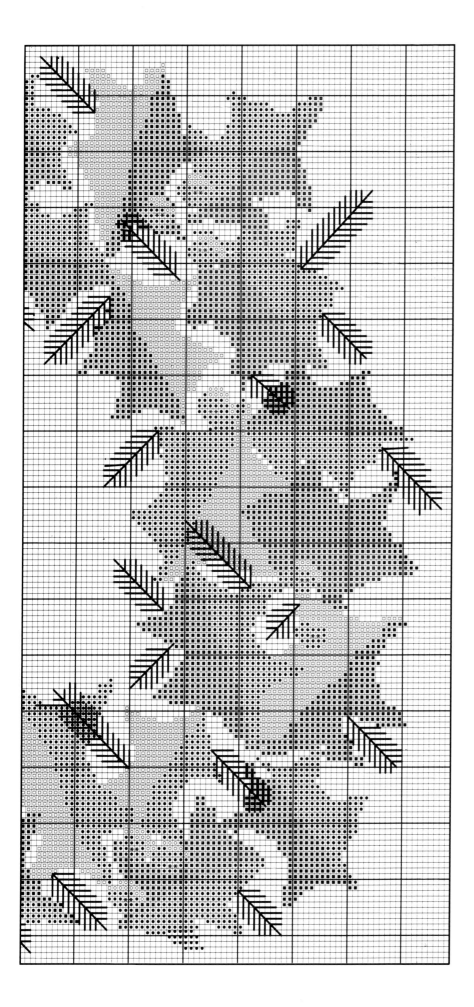

Beaded Rose Purse

Shimmering glass beads add a sophisticated touch to this elegant evening purse. Beads are applied simply by stitching them on waste canvas, using embroidery floss to match the background fabric. Use this design to embellish any number of wearables: stitch it to a shirt pocket, to an eyeglass case, or at the neckline of a favorite garment.

■ ■ ■ ■ ■ ■ ■ ■ ■ ■

SIZE: 9¼ × 7 inches (23.5 × 18cm); design area, 3½ × 2 inches (9 × 5cm)

FABRIC: Stitched using 16-count waste canvas on black velveteen

STITCH COUNT: 49 × 29

YOU WILL NEED:

- 16-count waste canvas, cut 6 × 5 inches (15 × 13cm)
- Six-strand black embroidery floss
- Mill Hill seed beads as listed in color key
- Tapestry needle size 24
- ⅜ yard (35.5cm) black cotton velveteen
- Black sewing thread
- ⅜ yard (35.5cm) lining fabric
- 2 yards (1.8m) ⅜-inch (1cm) black and gold twisted cording
- One pair black hook and loop tape circles
- One 12-inch (30.5cm) (or longer) black nylon zipper to match velvet
- Seam sealant

OPTIONS:

Fabric	Design Size
Aida 11	4½ × 2⅜ inches (11.5 × 6cm)
Aida 14	3½ × 2 inches (9 × 5cm)
Aida 18	2¾ × 1⅜ inches (7 × 3.5cm)

INSTRUCTIONS: Note: All seam allowances are ¼ inch (6mm).

Trace or photocopy the actual-size pattern for the purse flap. Cut out along the solid lines. Place the pattern on velveteen with the arrow corresponding to the nap of the fabric. Pin but do not cut out.

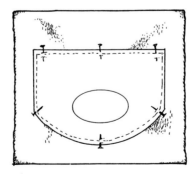

Cut a piece of waste canvas about 6 × 5 inches (15 × 13cm). Use the pattern to position the waste canvas, centering it where the beaded design will be worked.

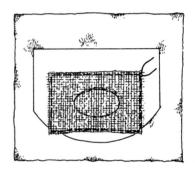

Remove the pins and pattern, and baste the edges of the waste canvas to the fabric. (Refer to chapter one for instructions on using waste canvas.) Stitch the beads in place (see page 16 for instructions) using two strands of floss and working over one thread of waste canvas. When you are finished stitching, remove the basting. Moisten the waste canvas and use tweezers to carefully pull each waste canvas thread from the stitching.

Cut out the placement window from the paper flap pattern. Center the flap pattern on the stitched velvet flap so that the window surrounds the beaded rose. Pin the pattern to the velveteen and cut along the outside edges of the pattern. Remove pattern. For the body of the purse, cut one velveteen rectangle $7\frac{1}{2} \times 10$ inches (19×25.5cm) for the front, and another 8×10 inches (20.5×25.5cm) for the back. From lining fabric, cut two rectangles, each $7\frac{1}{2} \times 10$ inches (19×25.5cm). Using the purse flap pattern, cut one flap from the velveteen for the inside of the purse flap.

Pin the two flap pieces together with right sides facing. Stitch $\frac{1}{4}$ inch (6mm) from edges, leaving the straight edges unstitched.

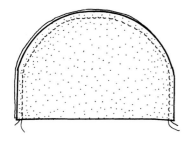

Clip into seam allowances, then turn right side out.

Leaving 1 inch (2.5cm) tails and starting at a corner, hand stitch twisted cord to the finished edge of the purse flap.

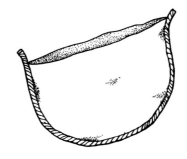

With right sides facing and edges even, pin and stitch zipper to one long edge of the purse back. The zipper will extend past one end of the rectangle; it will be trimmed later.

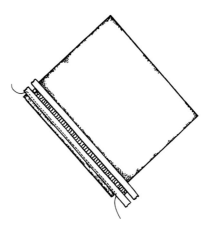

Make a $\frac{1}{4}$-inch (6m) -deep tuck in the fabric $\frac{1}{2}$ inch (1.5cm) from the zipper. Press.

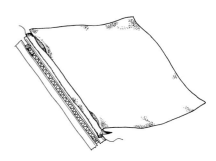

Make a $\frac{1}{2}$-inch (1.5cm) slit in the crease $\frac{1}{4}$ inch (6mm) in from each side edge as shown. Apply seam sealant to the slits. Insert the raw edges of the purse flap into the tuck as shown, and push the cord ends into the slits.

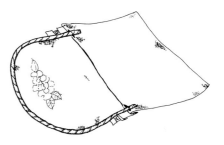

For a shoulder strap, insert ends of the remaining cord 1 inch (2.5cm) into the slits beside the flap cord ends. Stitch across cord ends to secure.

Fold the purse back over the flap so right sides are together. Stitch ¼ inch (6mm) from creased edge.

With right sides facing, pin and then stitch the purse front to the other side of the zipper.

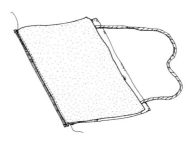

With wrong sides facing, stitch one long edge of each lining piece to each side of the zipper.

Open the zipper halfway. With right sides facing, pin the two lining pieces together and the two velveteen pieces together. With the teeth of the zipper

toward the velveteen, stitch all the way around the edges, leaving a 3-inch (6mm) opening along one side of the lining for turning.

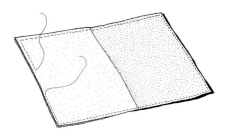

Trim away the extra length of zipper. Clip across corners. Turn purse right side out. Hand stitch the opening in the lining closed. Push the lining into the purse.

Hand stitch the hook and loop circles to the purse front and flap.

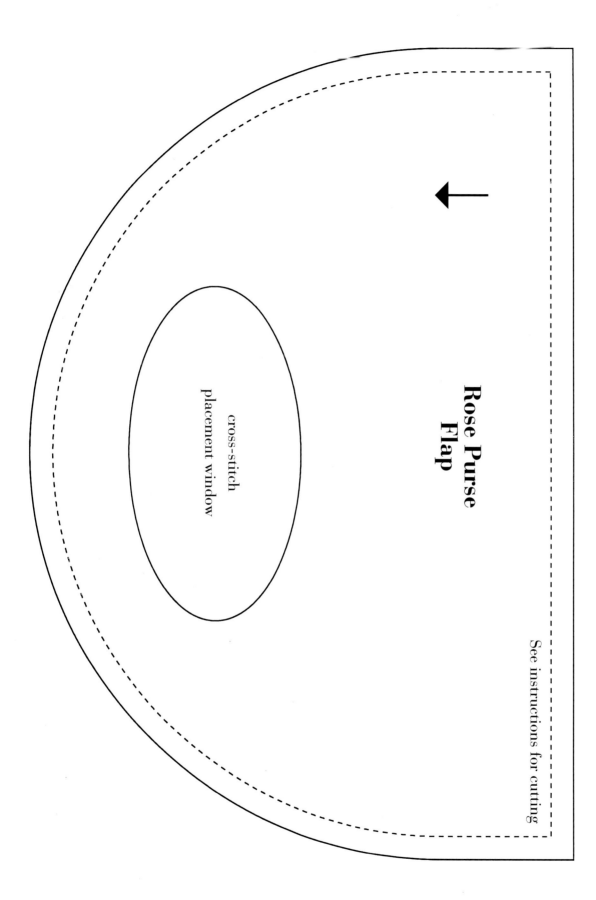

Rose Purse
Flap

cross-stitch
placement window

See instructions for cutting

Color Key

SYMBOL	MILL HILL SEED BEAD	COLOR
╱	00145	Pink
S	02002	Dusty Rose
□	00968	Red
B	00167	Christmas Green
+	00431	Jade
●	00332	Emerald

Stained Glass Angel

Hear the choir resound in celebration as your stitches bring this angel to life. Variegated floss (just one or two colors for each section) gives the stitchery depth, and blending filament gives it a glasslike effect.

▪ ▪ ▪ ▪ ▪ ▪ ▪ ▪ ▪ ▪ ▪

SIZE: Pillow, 13 × 15 inches (33 × 38cm), not including ruffle; design area, 7 ¼ × 11 ¾ inches (18.5 × 30cm)

FABRIC: Stitched on 28-count Dresden Blue Meran over two threads

STITCH COUNT: 100 × 160

YOU WILL NEED:

▪ 28-count Meran no. 3972 in Dresden blue from Zweigart, cut 15 × 18 inches (38 × 45.5cm)

▪ Six-strand embroidery floss as listed in color key, one skein each unless otherwise indicated

▪ Kreinik blending filament (BF) as listed in the color key, one spool each

▪ Mill Hill small bugle beads no. 72011, one package

▪ Tapestry needle size 26

▪ ¾ yard (68.5cm) 45-inch (114.5cm)-wide fabric for pillow backing and ruffle (here, plain taffeta)

▪ 13½ × 15½-inch (34.5 × 39.5cm) piece of muslin or other scrap fabric to line pillow top

▪ Matching sewing thread

▪ Polyester fiberfill for stuffing

▪ 2 yards (1.8m) soutouche ⅛-inch (3mm) braid

▪ 2 yards (1.8m) flat ⅜-inch (1cm) braid

▪ Seam sealant such as Fray Check

OPTIONS:

Fabric	Design Size
Aida 14	7⅛ × 11½ inches (18 × 29cm)
Aida 16	6 ¼ × 10 inches (16 × 25.5cm)
Aida 18	5½ × 8⅞ inches (14 × 22.5cm)
Linen 28	7⅛ × 11½ inches (18 × 29cm)

INSTRUCTIONS: Strip the floss and combine two strands so that the color gradations match (see page 10). Add the appropriate strand of blending filament as specified in the key. Stitch over two threads. To achieve the stained glass effect with the variegated thread, cross each stitch as you go. Add a strand of no. 028 blending filament rather than no. 005 for the black "leading" around the halo. Stitch the bugle beads over three threads above the candles as shown.

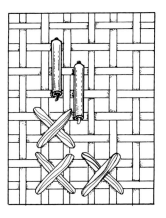

Make half cross-stitches for angel's mouth with light red floss, DMC 107.

PILLOW ASSEMBLY: Draw lines 3 inches (7.5cm) away from the ends of the outer black "leading" lines to all four edges of the pillow top. Cut. Seal the edges with seam sealant.

Draw lines on the pillow top as shown. Stitch the flat braid over the lines.

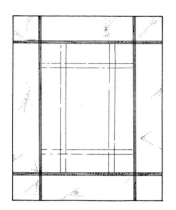

Baste the pillow top lining to the wrong side of the pillow top. Treat the two layers as one. From the backing and ruffle fabric, cut four 4-inch (10cm) -wide strips selvage to selvage for the ruffle, and one 13½ × 15½-inch (34.5 × 39.5cm) rectangle for the pillow backing. Sew the short ends of the ruffle pieces together to form a continuous ring. Fold one long edge ¼ inch (6mm) to the wrong side twice and topstitch. Sew a row of gathering stitches along the remaining long raw edge.

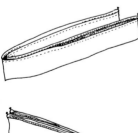

Fold the ruffle in half and in half again. Mark the four folds with pins. Match the pins to the centers of the four edges of the pillow top, right sides facing and raw edges even.

Pull thread ends to gather ruffle. Baste. Place the pillow top on the pillow back, with right sides facing, and ruffle in between. Leave a 6-inch (15cm) opening along the bottom edge for turning. Turn right side out. Stuff between the lining and the pillow back. Hand stitch the opening closed. Hand stitch the soutache to the outside edge of the cross-stitch fabric along the seam.

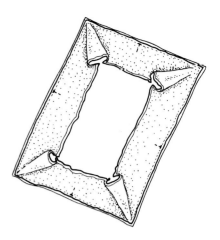

Color Key

SYMBOL	DMC V	BF	COLOR
Cross-stitch with 2 strands floss and 2 strands blending filament (see instructions):			
1	93	100	Blue, medium
●	111	100	Brown
+	115	031	Red, dark
%	52	012	Purple
8	107	031	Red, light
/	104	028	Yellow
▓	92	008	Moss Green
=	75	031	Red, medium
−	67	100	Blue, light
⊕	101	008	Kelly Green
□	1	100	White
B	310	005	Black
6	3774	100	Beige

Stained Glass Angel

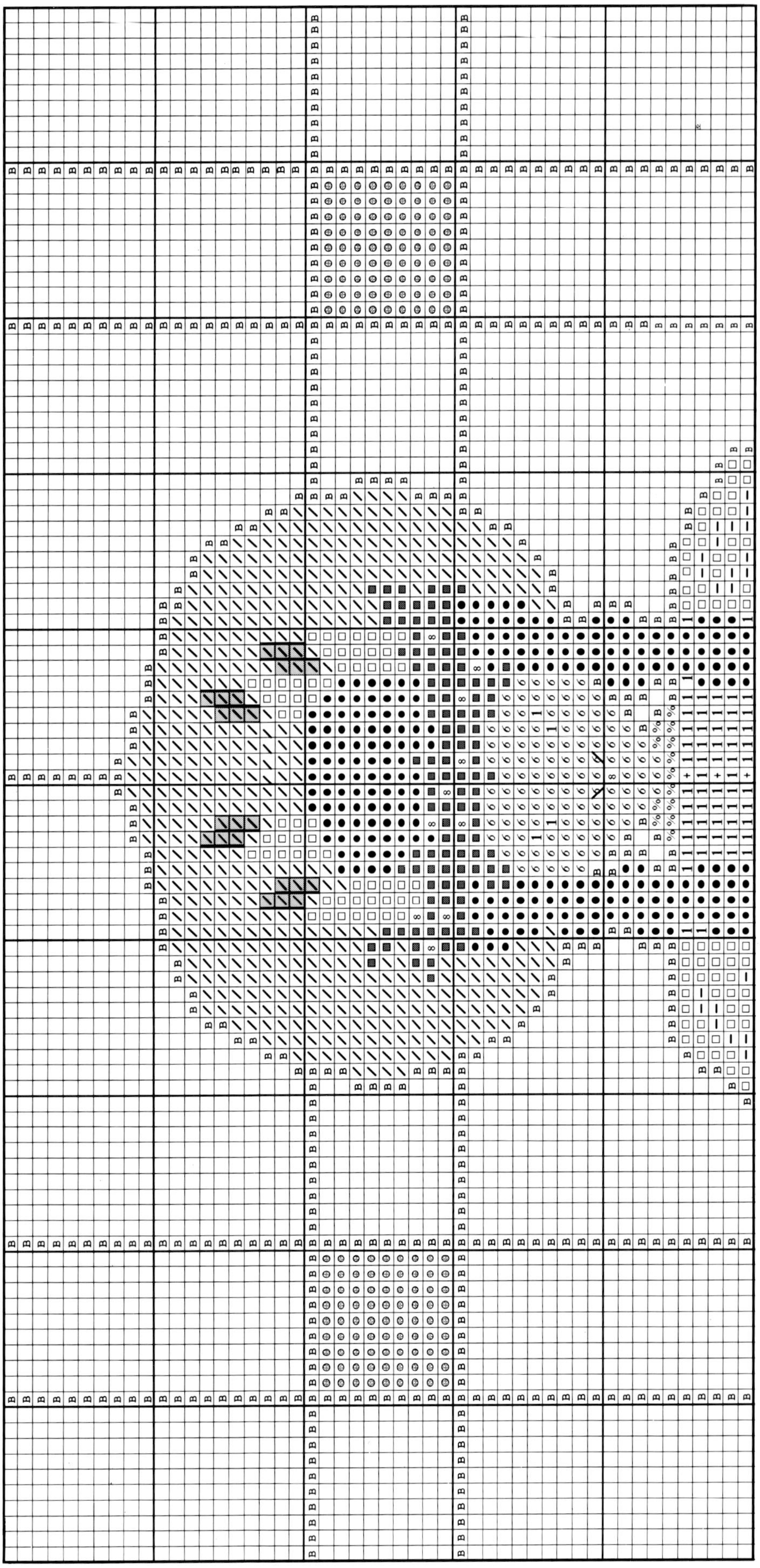

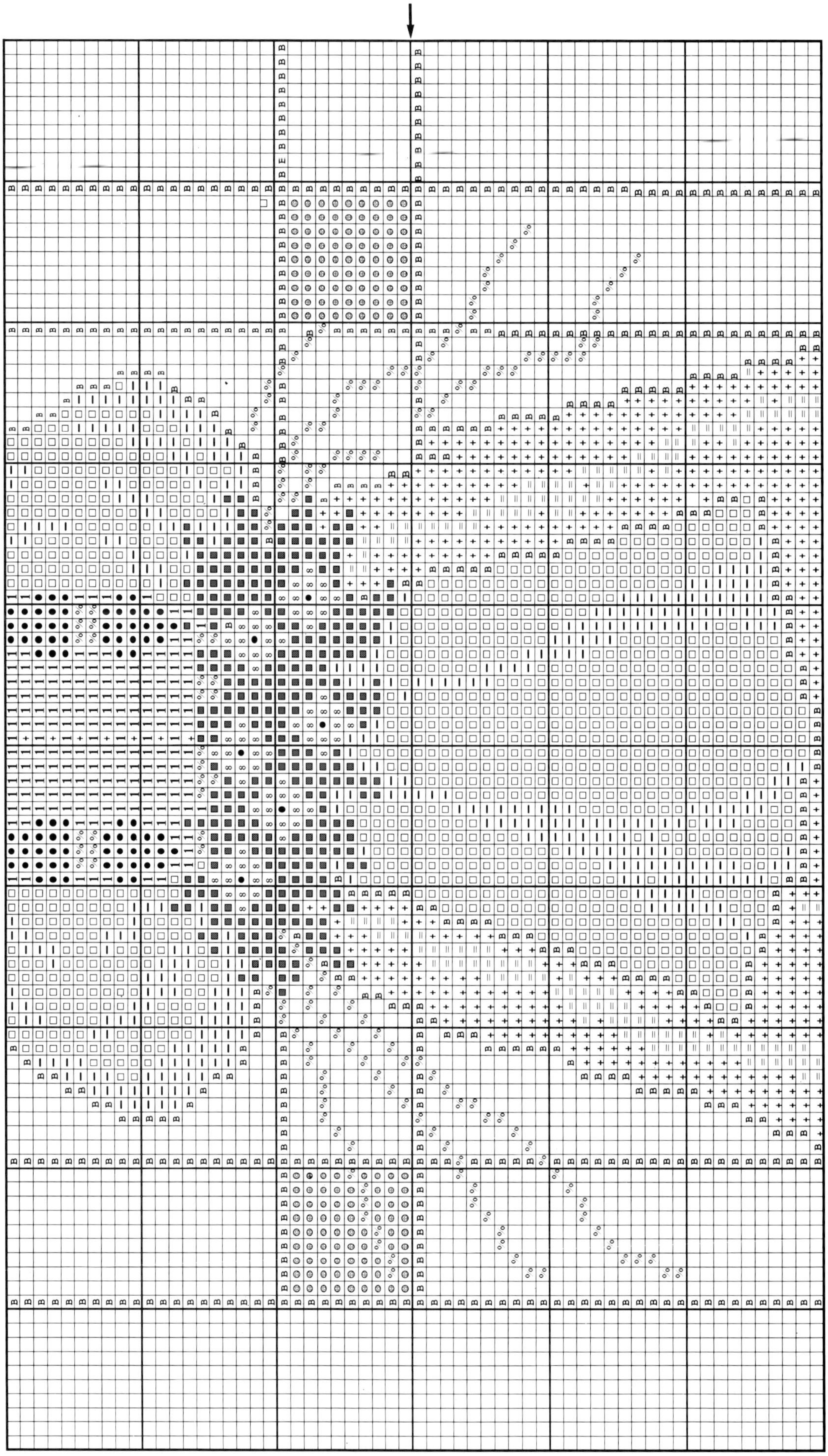

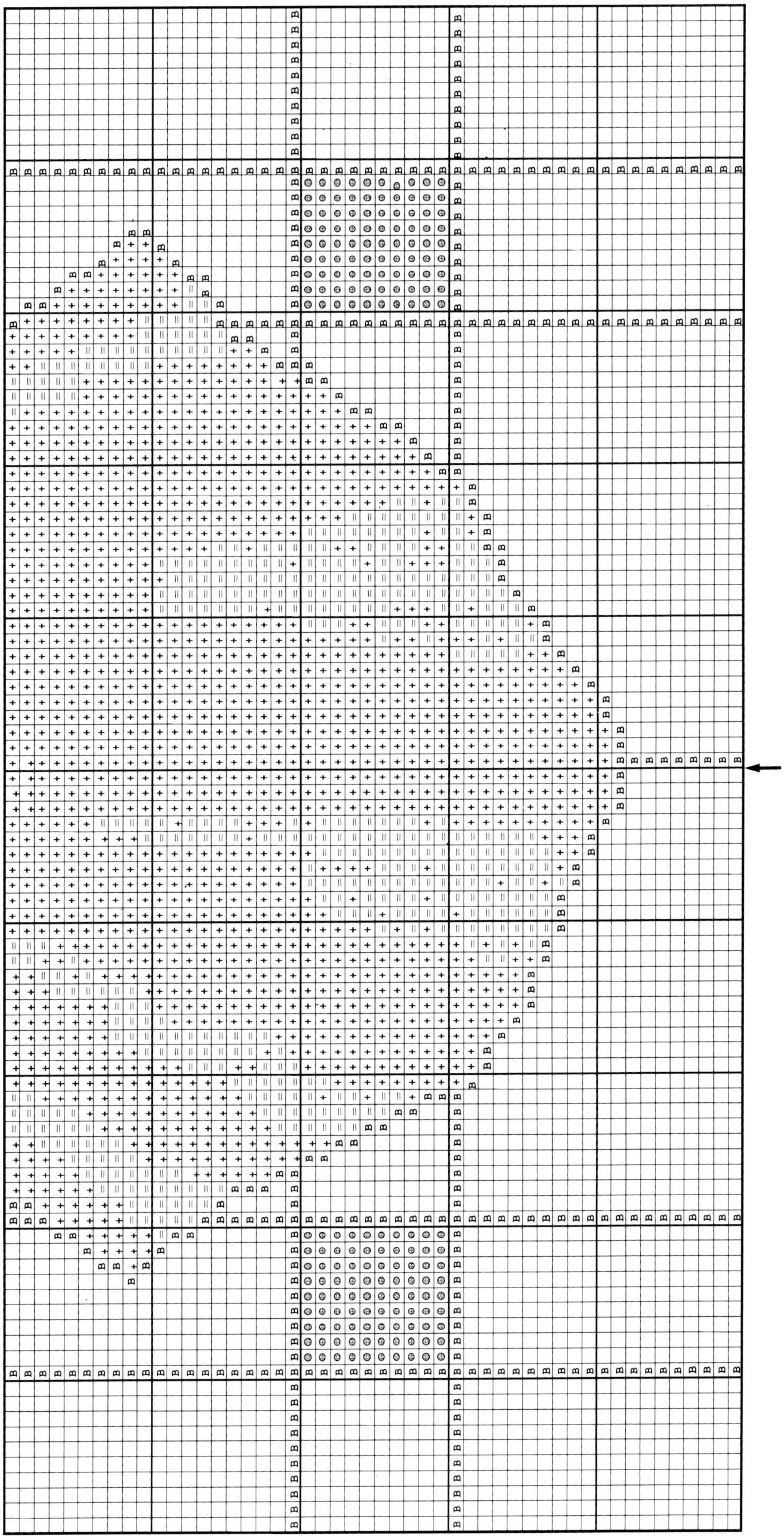

Snowflake Sampler

A subtly elegant white-on-white sampler offers the opportunity to try new stitches and specialty threads. Delicate beads and a crystal prism add extra sparkle.

■ ■ ■ ■ ■ ■ ■ ■

SIZE: Framed, $12\frac{1}{4} \times 13\frac{1}{3}$ inches (31×34 cm); design area, $5\frac{1}{4} \times 5\frac{1}{4}$ inches (13×13cm)

FABRIC: Stitched on 28-count white Cashel linen

STITCH COUNT: 73×83

YOU WILL NEED:

- 28-count white Cashel linen from Zweigart, cut 12 inches (30.5cm) square
- Six-strand white embroidery floss
- White pearl cotton no. 8
- White pearl cotton no. 12
- Kreinik blending filament no. 032
- Kreinik braid no. 3200
- Mill Hill bugle beads no. 0161
- Mill Hill small bugle beads no. 70161
- Mill Hill seed beads no. 0161
- Large snowflake crystal prism no. 718081CL from Needle Necessities (see Where to Find It)

OPTIONS:

Fabric	Design Size
Linen 25	$5\frac{7}{8} \times 6\frac{5}{8}$ inches (15×17cm)
Linen 30	$4\frac{7}{8} \times 5\frac{1}{2}$ inches (12.5×14cm)
Linen 22	$4\frac{1}{2} \times 5\frac{1}{4}$ inches (11.5×13cm)

INSTRUCTIONS: Stitch following the stitching key and stitch illustrations. Refer to page 16 for bead stitching instructions. Following is the Algerian eyelet stitch:

In the gray area of the chart, plot your monogram. (Refer to the Berry Sampler on pages 64 and 65 for alphabetical numerals.) Stitch your initials and the date in the space left on the chart. After washing and pressing, sew crystal prism so it hangs between initials and date.

FRAMING OPTION: Insert in a frame with a $10\frac{1}{2} \times 11\frac{1}{2}$-inch ($26.5 \times 29$cm) opening. Create an inner frame with narrow molding, and mat and frame with a wide molding to match.

Stitching Key

Band 1	Herringbone	Pearl cotton no. 8
Band 2	Cross-stitch	Combine 2 strands white floss and 2 strands Kreinik Blending Filament no. 032
		Seed beads no. 032 at point of each "icicle"
Band 3	Herringbone stitch	Pearl cotton no. 8
Band 4	Algerian eyelet	no. 12 Pearl cotton stitch
Band 5	Herringbone stitch	Pearl cotton no. 8
Band 6	Eyelet variation	2 strands white floss
Band 7	Satin stitch	Pearl cotton no. 8
Band 8	Cross-stitch	2 strands white floss
		Small bugle beads no. 70161
		Seed beads no. 0161
Band 9	Satin stitch	Pearl cotton no. 8
Band 10	Cross-stitch	Combine 2 strands white floss and 2 strands Kreinik Blending Filament no. 032
		Seed beads no. 032
Band 11	Long arm cross-stitch	Pearl cotton no. 8
Band 12	Half cross-stitch	1 strand Kreinik no. 3200 braid
		Seed beads no. 0161
Band 13	Long arm cross-stitch	Pearl cotton no. 8

Snowflake Sampler

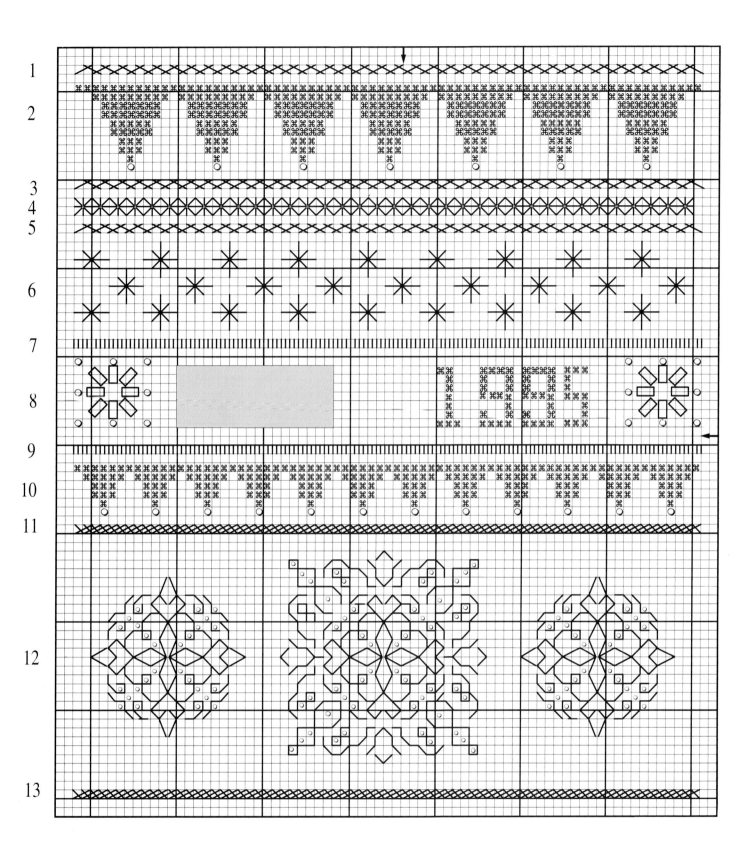

A Sampling of
Small Accessories

. . .

The motifs for these projects are adapted from the samplers shown previously. But there's no need to limit yourself to these designs—any small pictorial may be considered for a miniature masterpiece. Refer to the sampler project where the motif originally appeared for fabric type, tapestry needle size, and instructions for stitching.

Heart Charm

. . .

SIZE: 3 inches (7.5cm)

YOU WILL NEED:

- Same fabric as for sampler, cut 8 × 8 inches (20.5 × 20.5cm)
- Threads as listed in color key
- Medium heart charm and bow pin with safety catch from Pat & Pam (see Where to Find It)
- ³/₈ yard (35.5cm) twisted braid (optional)
- Same tapestry needle as for sampler

INSTRUCTIONS: See chosen sampler for stitching instructions; refer to manufacturer's instructions for assembly.

Optional: After assembling the charm, hand stitch the twisted cord along the edges. Overlap the ends and hide the raw edges on the back.

Key Ring

. . .

SIZE: 4 × 2 ¹/₈ inches (10 × 5.5cm)

YOU WILL NEED:

- Same fabric as for sampler, cut 6 × 8 inches (15 × 20.5cm)
- Threads as listed in color key
- Acrylic Bag Tag/Key Ring no. BT01 from Fond Memories (see Where to Find It)
- Fusible interfacing
- Same tapestry needle as for sampler

INSTRUCTIONS: See chosen sampler for stitching instructions; refer to manufacturer's instructions for assembly.

Optional: Surround a small motif with a bow of ¹/₄-inch (6mm) -wide satin ribbon, tacked gracefully into place.

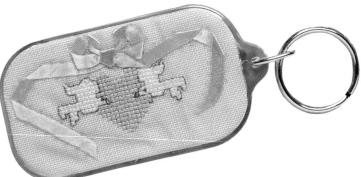

$\mathcal{C}$oasters

. . .

SIZE: $3\frac{1}{2}$ inches (9cm)

YOU WILL NEED:

- Same fabric as for sampler, cut 6 × 8 inches (15 × 20.5cm)
- Threads as listed in color key
- Acrylic coaster no. C01 from Fond Memories (see Where to Find It)
- Same tapestry needle as for sampler

INSTRUCTIONS: See chosen sampler for stitching instructions; refer to manufacturer's instructions for assembly.

$\mathcal{B}$ookmark

. . .

SIZE: $3\frac{1}{4} \times 6\frac{1}{2}$ inches (8 × 16.5cm)

YOU WILL NEED:

- Same fabric as for sampler, cut 5 × 8 inches (13 × 20.5 cm)
- Threads as listed in color key
- Sewing thread to match fabric
- Same tapestry needle as for sampler

INSTRUCTIONS: See chosen sampler for stitching instructions. Cross-stitch design to center of fabric.

Mark and cut a $3\frac{1}{4} \times 6\frac{5}{8}$-inch (8 × 17cm) rectangle around the stitched design. Machine stitch all the way around, $\frac{1}{2}$ inch (1.5 cm) from the raw edges. Fringe the raw edges by removing threads up to the stitching.

Scroll Pin

...

SIZE: $3\frac{5}{8} \times 3$ inches (9×7.5cm)

YOU WILL NEED:

- Same fabric as for sampler, cut 8×8 inches (20.5×20.5cm)
- Threads as listed in color key
- Four $\frac{7}{32} \times \frac{1}{4}$-inch ($5.5 \times 6$mm) axle peg wood turnings from Darice
- Plastic drinking straw
- Hand sewing thread to match the fabric
- Pin
- White glue
- Same tapestry needle as for sampler

INSTRUCTIONS: See chosen sampler for stitching instructions. Mark and cut a 3×5-inch (7.5×13cm) rectangle around the stitched design. Fold the two long edges $\frac{1}{4}$ inch (6mm) to the back.

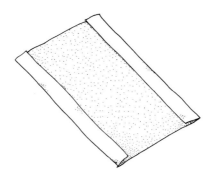

From a plastic drinking straw, cut two $2\frac{1}{2}$-inch (6.5cm) -long pieces. Apply a small amount of glue to wooden axles and insert into each open end of straw.

Place the straw/axles on the wrong side of the fabric. Fold $\frac{3}{4}$ inch (2cm) fabric over the straw, to the back. Stitch through both layers of fabric, below the straw.

Roll the axle to the front slightly to cover the stitching. Tack with tiny stitches to hold in place. Trim away excess fabric at the back.

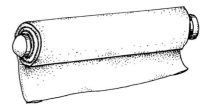

Repeat for other end. Glue or stitch pin back to back of fabric, near the top edge.

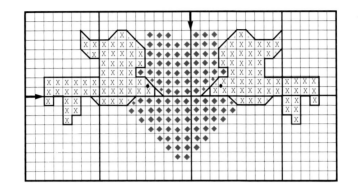

Dove Sampler Motif Color Key

SYMBOL	DMC	ANCHOR	COATS	COLOR
Cross-stitch with 1 strand over 2 threads :				
X	White	2	1001	White
◈	209	109	4303	Lavender, dark
Backstitch with 1 strand:				
╱	3022	393	5393	Brown-gray, medium (dove)
French knots with 1 strand:				
●	3022	393	5393	Brown-gray, medium (dove eyes)

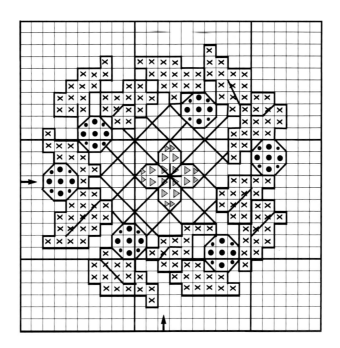

Berry Sampler Motif Color Key

SYMBOL	DMC	DMC VARIEGATED	CW	COLOR
Cross-stitch with 2 strands over 2 threads:				
●		012		Wildberries
✗		122		Green
△	Ecru			Ecru
Backstitch with 1 strand:				
—	987			Forest Green, dark (leaves and berries)
—	301			Mahogany, medium (flower, cross-hatching, and dove eyes)

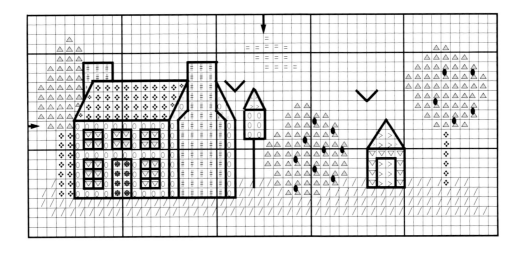

Village Sampler Motif Color Key

SYMBOL	DMC FLOWER THREAD	CW	COLOR
Cross-stitch with 1 strand over 2 threads:			
❖	2898		Brown
#	2354		Brick
>	2319		Green
▽	2743		Yellow, light
▲	2890		Green, dark
❁	2322		Country Blue
0	White		White
Half cross-stitch with 1 strand:			
/		065	Emerald
French knots with 1 strand:			
●	2321		Red (apples)
Backstitch with 1 strand:			
—	2898		Brown (roof, windows, shutters, and door)
—	White		White (house and bird-house)
—	2890		Green, dark (outhouse roof and door)
—	2310		Black (birdhouse pole)
—	2354		Brick (chimney)
—	2825		Blue, medium (birds)

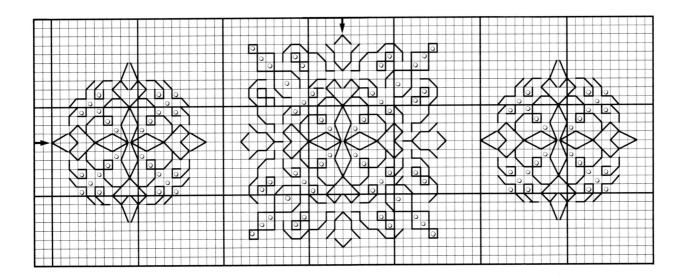

Snowflake Sampler Motif Color Key

MATERIAL

Half cross-stitch with 1 strand and beads over 2 threads:

    1 strand Kreinik no. 3200 braid

    Seed beads no. 0161

A Summary of Stitching Instructions

You Are Invited...

To me crafts are about sharing. It brings me great pleasure to share my designs with you and I hope you will enjoy stitching them as much as I have enjoyed the magical process of making my ideas come to life.

In this spirit I invite you to share your creations through the mail. Tell me about yourself and your cross-stitch projects, as well as any other crafts you enjoy. Whether you use my patterns as is, adapt them for your own purposes, or create your own designs, I look forward to meeting you by mail.

Jodie Davis

Jodie Davis Publishing, Inc.
15 West 26 Street
New York, NY 10010

or via CompuServe: 73522,2430
    GEnie: J.Davis60

Appendix: Where to Find It
. . .

Your local needlecrafts store will have most of the materials for making the projects in this book. If you need an item that your store doesn't carry, they will most likely be happy to order it for you. Check local listings for a needlecrafts store near you or contact the manufacturer of the item you need for a list of stores that carry their products. For those of you who find it difficult to get to a shop, I have included some excellent mail-order sources.

Aleene's
85 Industrial Way
Buellton, CA 93427
(805) 688-7339
(800) 436-7878
Fax (800) 688-8638

The Caron Collection
67 Poland Street
Bridgeport, CT 06605
(800) 862-2766

Charles Craft
P.O. Box 1049
Laurinburg, NC 28353
(800) 277-0980

Coats & Clark
30 Patewood Drive
Suite 351
Greenville, SC 29615
(803) 234-0331

The DMC Corporation
Port Kearny
Building #10
South Kearny, NJ 07032
(800) 688-8362

Fairfield Processing Corporation
P.O. Box 1157
Danbury, CT 06813
(800) 243-0989

Fond Memories, Inc.
One Terminal Way
Norwich, CT 06360
(203) 887-4789
(800) 456-1021

Gay Bowles Sales, Inc.
1310 Plainfield Avenue
P.O. Box 1060
Janesville, WI 53547
(608) 754-9466

Kreinik Mfg Co., Inc.
P.O. Box 1966
Parkersburg, WV 26101
(800) 624-1928

Needle Necessities, Inc.
14746 N.E. 95th Street
Redmond, WA 98052
(206) 881-2161
(800) 542-7300

Pat & Pam

P.O. Box 5008
Lubbock, TX 79408
(806) 792-0844
(800) 766-0844

The Rainbow Gallery

7412 Fulton Avenue #5
North Hollywood, CA 91605
(818) 982-6406
(800) 522-6827

Reed Baxter Woodcrafts, Inc.

P.O. Box 2186
Eugene, OR 97402
Phone/fax (503) 683-1210
Orders (800) 327-7338

Sudberry House

Box 895
Old Lyme, CT 06371
(203) 739-6951

Tomorrow's Treasures

19722 144th Avenue, N.E.
Woodinville, WA 98072
(206) 487-2636
(800) 882-8932

Wichelt Fabrics

Wichelt Imports, Inc.
Rural Route 1
Stoddard, WI 54648
(608) 788-4600

The Woodshaper Co.

P.O. Box 335
Hamer, SC 29547
(803) 774-3192
(800) 367-5271

Zweigart Fabrics

Zweigart/Joan Toggitt Ltd.
Weston Canal Plaza
2 Riverview Drive
Somerset, NJ 08873
(908) 271-1949

IN CANADA:

Coats Patons Canada

1001 Roselawn Ave.
Toronto, Ontario M6B 1B8
(416) 782-4481

The Siver Thimble, Inc.

64 Rebecca Steet
Oakville, Ontario L6U 1U2
(905) 845-6461

ALL FRAMING BY:

Jannette Jackson

Old Town Needlecrafts
9774 Center Street
Manassas, VA 22110
(703) 330-1846

MAIL-ORDER SOURCES

*Cross Stitch &
Country Crafts*

Catalog Dept.
111 Tenth Street
P.O. Box 11447
Des Moines, IA 50309
(800) 678-2694 (Credit card
orders only)
Catalog: $2.00

Color catalog of cross-stitch charts,
kits, and supplies.

*Mary Jane's Cross
'N' Stitch*

5120 Belmont Road
Downers Grove, IL 60515

(708) 963-9678
Fax (708) 963-9679
(800) 334-6819
Catalog: $7.25 UPS delivery;
includes a $5 credit coupon for
your first order of $25 or more

This informative catalog arrives in
a three-ring binder, ready for peri-
odic updates. Provides an excellent
selection of cross-stitch supplies
and charts.

Nordic Needle

1314 Gateway Drive
Fargo, ND 58103
(701) 235-5231
Fax (701) 235-0952
(800) 433-4321
Catalog: Free

An exhaustive catalog of cross-stitch
supplies. Carries a large selection of
specialty threads as well as more
common ones. Also carries cross-
stitch accessories.

The Stitchery

120 N. Meadows Road
Medfield, MA 02052-1592
Customer service (800) 688-8051
Orders (800) 388-9662

Color catalog of needlework kits.

BIBLIOGRAPHY

O'Steen, Darleen. *The Proper Stitch: A Guide for Counted Thread.*
   Excellence Publishers, Inc., 1994.

Thompson, Ginnie. *Linen Stitches.* Designs by Gloria & Pat, Inc., 1987.

Toth, Cecilia, ed. *The Good Housekeeping Book of Needlecrafts.*
   Hearst Books, 1994.

Van Zandt, Eleanor. *Reader's Digest Complete Book of Cross Stitch
   and Counted Thread Techniques.* Collins & Brown, Limited, 1994.

Index
• • •

A

Accessories, 112–116
   Beaded Rose Purse, *92*, 93–95
   Bookmark, *114*, 117
   Coasters, *114*, 117
   Heart Charm, *114*, 116
   Key Ring, *114*, 116
   Scroll Pin, *114*, 118
Angels, 102–107

B

Beads, 16, 47
   bugle, 103, 109
   glass, 97
   seed, 58, 97, 109
Blending filament, 11, 103
Braid, 109
Buttons, 58

C

Canvas, waste, 12, 97
Christmas projects
   Christmas Wreath, *92*, 93–95
   Snowflake Sampler,
     108, 109–111
   Stained Glass Angel,
     102, 103–107

F

Fabrics, 11–12, 15
   drying, 17
   finishing, 16–17
   preparation, 13
   raveling, 13
   stiffener, 56–57
Fiberfill, 47, 83, 103
Floss, 10–11
   blending filament, 11, 103, 109
   color bleeding, 11
   Flower, 83
   hand-dyed, 11, 47, 63, 83
   metallic, 27, 71

   specialty, 11
   strands, 10
   variegated, 11, 47, 63,
     79, 83, 103
Frames, 13, 17
   arch cut, 39
   double mat, 20, 30, 39, 44, 68,
     79, 90, 93
   triple mat, 63, 75, 93
French knots, 16, 56–57, 63, 83

H

Hoops, 13

I

Instructions
   Autumn Landscape, 68
   Beaded Rose Purse, 97
   Berry Sampler, 63
   Bookmark, 115
   Butterfly Lamp, 27
   Christmas Wreath, 93

Coasters, 115

Dove Sampler, 39

Harvest Welcome Wreath, 75

Heart Charm, 116

Key Ring, 116

Kitty in a Window, 55

Peppers wall chart, 71

Quilt Baskets, 79

Quilt Design Pillows, 47–49

Quilt Sign, 30

Scroll Pin, 116

Snowflake Sampler, 109

Spring Landscape, 20

Stained Glass Angel, 103–104

Summer Landscape, 44

Victorian Porch, 58

Village Sampler, 83

Winter Landscape, 90

Woodland Wildflowers, 23

Interfacing, 116

L

Lamps, 26–29, *26*

N

Needles, 12–13

P

Paper, perforated, 12

Patterns

Autumn Landscape, 69

Beaded Rose Purse, 97–99

Berry Sampler, 64–65

Butterfly Lamp, 28–29

Christmas Wreath, 94–95

Dove Sampler, 40–41

Harvest Welcome Wreath, 76–77

Irish Chain Quilt, 36

Kitty in a Window, 56–57

Peppers wall chart, 72–73

Quilt Baskets, 81

Quilt Design Pillows, 50–53

Quilt Signs, 32–37

Schoolhouse Quilt, 35

Snowflake Sampler, 111

Spring Landscape, 21

Summer Landscape, 45

Trip 'Round the World Quilt, 37

Victorian Porch, 60–61

Village Sampler, 85–87

Winter Landscape, 91

Woodland Wildflowers, 24–25

Pillows, *46, 48, 49*

assembly, 47–49, 83, 103–104

forms for, 47

Quilt Design, 46–53

Stained Glass Angel,

102, 103–107

stuffing, 47

Village Sampler, *82,* 83–87

Projects

accessories, 114–117

angels, 102–107

autumn, 66–87

butterflies, 26–29

Christmas, 92–95, 102–107

flower, 22–25

lamps, 26–29

pillows, 46–53, *82,* 83–87

purses, 96–101

samplers, 38–41, 62–65, *82,*

83–87, 108–111

spring, 18–41

summer, 42–65

winter, 88–111

wreaths, *74,* 75–77, *92,* 93–95

Purses, 96–101

S

Samplers

Berry Sampler, 62–65

Dove Sampler, 38–41

Snowflake Sampler, *108,*

109–111

Village Sampler, *82,* 83–87

white-on-white, *108,* 109–111

Seam sealant, 11, 47, 97, 103

Stitches

    Algerian eyelet, 109

    backstitch, 16, 63, 71, 79, 83

    beginning, 14

    carrying threads, 15

    four-sided, 79

    French knot, 16, 56–57, 63, 83

    lazy daisy, 83

    loop method, 14

    pulled, 83

    running backstitch, 83

    stab, 15

    waste knot method, 14

    working over the thread tail
        method, 14

Supplies and materials, 10

    Autumn Landscape, 68

    Beaded Rose Purse, 97

    Berry Sampler, 63

    Bookmark, 115

    Butterfly Lamp, 27

    Christmas Wreath, 93

    Coasters, 115

    Dove Sampler, 38

    Harvest Welcome Wreath, 75

    Heart Charm, 116

    Key Ring, 116

    Kitty in a Window, 55

    Peppers wall chart, 71

Quilt Baskets, 79

Quilt Design Pillows, 47

Quilt Sign, 30

Scroll Pin, 116

Snowflake Sampler, 109

Spring Landscape, 20

Stained Glass Angel, 103

Summer Landscape, 44

Victorian Porch, 58

Village Sampler, 83

Winter Landscape, 90

Woodland Wildflowers, 23

T

Thread. *See* Floss.

W

Wall decor

    Autumn Landscape, *66*, 68–69

    Berry Sampler, 62–65, *62*

    Christmas Wreath, *92*, 93–95

    Dove Sampler, 38–41, *38*

    Harvest Welcome Wreath, *74*,
        75–77

    Kitty in a Window, 54–57

    Peppers, *70*, 71–73

    Quilt Baskets, *78*, 79–81

    Quilt Sign, 30–37, *30*

    Snowflake Sampler, *108*,
        109–111

Spring Landscape, *18*, 20–21

Summer Landscape, *42*, 44–45

Victorian Porch, 58–61, *59*

Village Sampler, *82*, 83–87

Winter Landscape, 88, 90–91

Woodland Wildflowers, 22–25, *22*

Wreaths, *74*, 75–77